Follow Your Heart

B&W edition

*"This above all: to thine own self be true
and thus it must follow
as night the day;
thou canst not then be false to any man."*
Wm. Shakespeare

Journeys into the Soul trilogy

Follow your Heart
My physical journeys following a vision of God.

Drops of Rain and Grains of Sand
Affirmations of learning following the same vision.

God is out, please take a seat in the waiting room
My own understanding of god/God.

Follow Your Heart

A Story of Miracles, Magic and One Man's Adventure

Michael Fleming/Brahmacharya Baba

All of the stories in this work are true and the people are real although most of the names have been changed.

First published in color – 2013
Published in Black and White - 2018

First Published by Michaels Rainbow

Copyright © 2013
by Michael Fleming/Brahmacharya Baba
All rights reserved.

ISBN: 978-0-9910130-3-6

Printed in the United States of America

ACKNOWLEDGMENTS

Special thanks to Steve Hoffmann, who liked me and my work enough to struggle through the first very rough draft - and in so doing, taught me many things.

Gregory Zabilski for the back cover portrait of me and for technical support with the photographic images.

To Doctor Peter Milhado, who helped me to face the truth.

Daniel Rover Singer for the Hamlet drawing.

John Coffey for the photo of Styx.

Thanks also to
Debbie Christensen, Ronni Sanlo, Marie Larsen (Red) and Dan Kugle.

Thanks to Mark Miny
who told me that he wanted to know more about the people in the book.

Cover and photography by Michael Fleming

Special thanks to all the others who have helped and guided me through the maze that is self publishing.

A few notes from friends
who have previewed my book:

"Wow! What amazes me most is that you actually remember the various visions you had in such vivid detail. My recollection does not vary that much from yours. You once went into that catatonic state for so long I didn't think I would ever get you back out again. I just held you in my arms for 30 minutes or more until you finally struggled back from wherever you had been. Sometimes you hear something and it doesn't really 'register' until you emotionalize it, which you certainly DID under acid."
-- Jon Michael, Bradfordsville, Kentucky

Genius!!!!
-- Claire Sarradet, Quebec, Canada

I have just finished reading your book. Such bold narration of the journey of life indeed calls for guts. Description of various events are marvelous. The book reveals your strong character, your honesty and power of your pen. You have achieved a state of mind, as it appears, which we Hindu's call "Nirvana." (I) Wish you many more years of "Self-realization." Keep following your heart!
-- Bibhash Bhaduri (Khokon), Varanasi, India

I have read your transcript and was blown away from its content. I found it to be so many things and it renewed my hope, faith, energy and ability to see the world from fresh eyes. [It] renewed my goal to see the best in all things and people! Thank you.
Betty Rodola-Prock, Dana Point, California

Originally, only think speak and listen to enough. But just speak and listen already insufficient now. The story that you write has philosophic truth very much so I need slowly read several times. You have changed my life, teacher. I enjoy this story so learning goes deep, I will continue to travel with your story. You give me much energy. I can do anything.
    -- Chiu wu-chung 邱武忠, Taoyuan County, Taiwan

Dearest Brahmacharya Baba Ji, Pranam,
I am touched by some of the sentences which appear to be simple but have deep philosophical realization. Now, realization of God! It is difficult,-if not impossible,-to feel, to realize, the God; but your vision of God after "acid" has its own piety and love.
    -- Soumitra Basu, New Delhi, India

These tales leaven my afternoons so well. I am SO enjoying this book! "There are few people with whom I have remained in communication as I have changed from one life to another." You're probably the only person I've ever met for whom that makes perfect sense. You didn't just move from one job to another or one house to another; you really did go from one LIFE to another. I enjoyed your story more than just about anything I've read in the last few years; and I do read lots and lots and lots. It's my favorite pastime. Thank you so much for sharing it with me.
    And what a TOTALLY SATISFYING ENDING!
    -- Steve Hoffmann, Anoka, Minnesota

When I was very young, I asked my Sunday school teacher,
    who I was sure knew God
        (as I would when I grew up),
"Which should I follow (should I ever have to choose),
    THE CHURCH or my heart?"
        She told me to follow my heart.

            To her, I dedicate this writing.

Chapter 1

Acid Trips and Seeing God

The 1960s and 70s were a very powerful time for many people. Conventional ways of living were being challenged by change, and old ideas by new ways of thinking. People with very good jobs simply quit and walked away. Many with friends and families "stepped out" and became free from it all. They became "Flower Children" or "Hippies."

It was a time of finding One's Self. Love and freedom were the messages of the hippies. They were balanced by the war in Viet Nam, and the dawning of the Age of Aquarius. New thought entered the world at that time. Those who heard the messages were changed forever.

I was living with Jon. We had a big house overlooking Silver Lake reservoir in Los Angeles, California. We had lived, loved and grown together for four years. There came a time when we were to part. His pathway was leading him to become an executive while mine would lead into an entirely different life;
- - and this story.

At the time I was a successful computer programmer working for Sears Roebuck & Co. Jon was on his way up the ladder in purchasing; he ended up being in charge of Sears, Asia.

We had a mutual friend named Marshall, who also worked with Jon, and both of them worked on the same floor as me, so this is how the three of us met.

Marshal and I seemed to share an intimacy of some sort with each other and we became close friends. One day Marshall told me that he had taken LSD, called "acid." He wanted us to try it with him. I did know that acid was around but had never tried it and was reluctant to do so, but he praised it so much that I said I would try. Jon and I both decided to try it with Marshall and planned a special night to take "the trip." As fate would have it, on the day we had planned for our acid trip, the Sears computer system in San Francisco had a problem with a program that I had written.

I had to fly to Northern California to resolve the problem. Anxiously I worked to correct the program so I could catch a plane home in time. I was afraid I would be too late. I had become very eager to do this acid thing. Somehow, I knew that this was something I had to do. I wanted to make this a very special night. As I was flying back home, I was planning everything in my mind. I knew I was going through something very powerful in my life. As I flew back home I felt like I was flying from one life into another.

Arriving home, I rushed into the house to make it gentle and calm with candles, incense and soft music. I made a fire; we were told that we would be cold (and I've never liked being cold). Different kinds of food and fruits; we were also told that we would get the munchies. Jon and I were really excited about doing this forbidden thing, well, at

least I was. Setting ourselves up with fresh fruit and good food and with the music of Ravi Shankar, we began a voyage that was to change my life. Throwing my suitcase into the bedroom, I settled into a long, hot bath. I needed to prepare myself as well. Calmness was what was needed now.
We took the pill.

I felt nothing at first then, "Oh God!" I suddenly felt more apprehensive than I had ever felt before. I did not know what was coming, but I knew there was nothing I could do about it. I had so many prejudices and so many doubts, but I was really trying to stay calm. I was paranoid and began shaking violently. The haunting music of Ravi Shankar playing the sitar with long vibrating sounds found its way inside my head, the vibrations of the strings finding resonance within my soul. I could feel the music drawing me somewhere. Resisting because of fear—letting go came hard for me—I was drawn to the sounds of the sitar just the same.

After a time, I calmed down. We were sitting on the floor in front of the fireplace and I found myself looking into Marshall's eyes. I could see paisley patterns all around, superimposed mostly on faces. Everything and everyone radiated with these beautiful patterns. The emotional vibrations of the music seemed to be leading me deeper into Marshall's eyes.

Then an image appeared midway between us in front of his face. It contained him, yet there was more. It also reflected me, a combined image of both of us. I was drawn deeply into the image. I could see and experience feelings there. I thought I was seeing Marshall's image. The vision showed me a person who gave, but did not love. I loved Marshall and did not want to tell him what I had seen. Yet, I knew that I had to tell him somehow.

Crying from my heart I said, "Marshall, I have seen something in you that I have to tell you and it hurts so badly to have to say it." He in turn, was crying as he said, "You too, Mike, I have seen something about you that I have to tell you, and I want so much not to tell you because I don't want to hurt you either." We hugged each other and cried, wishing that we did not have to tell what we had seen. Finally, through our love, we did tell.

"Marshall," I said, "You don't love." I sobbed. The sorrow was sounding deep within me. Marshall looked at me and, crying as well, told me what he had seen, whatever it was. As I said the words, "You don't love," it became clear that the vision I had been looking at had been a reflection of myself. It was me who did not love. I was looking at ME! What Marshall had seen was also a personal reflection of himself. The sadness that I had felt for Marshall not loving was really sadness at my own inability to love.

It was from this vision that I learned that I am reflected in all that I see.

I did not love. Nope, that was me in a nutshell; I did not know how to love. It was just not something that I had grown up with.

My own mother told me that she had not loved me at first. She even told me once that she was too busy providing food and clothing to give me love; and I had steeled myself away from this emotion. To give her credit she was working for the war effort when I was very young. It was during the Second World War. She worked about 30 miles from home; she took the bus to the train station and went to work on the train. Then take the train and local bus home; cook dinner, do some cleaning and often had her friends over during the evening. She kept a clean and stable house. She had two kids who got looked after by a really neat old lady who lived next door, "Aunt Blanch."

We had all that we needed; just no love.

I was young and not unattractive. Several times over the years, I had dated guys who fell in love with me. "I won't love you," I would tell them, "it's nothing personal, I just don't know how to love."

Then I saw a flash. It appeared to me like a star in a dark sky. Fascinated, I allowed myself to be drawn to this star.

I was running home from school; I was being chased. The church was directly in front of me. I ran inside and hid behind the curtains on the stage in the recreation room-Her name was Annette, she had pig-tails as I remember and she was chasing me for some reason and I simply didn't know how to respond to her anger, or whatever it was that she was feeling toward me, so I ran and hid. She didn't find me although she did look. Barely breathing, I stood without moving behind the drapes.

"Mike," a voice intruded into my reverie. "Where are you?"

"I'm in church, hiding behind the drapes," I replied.

I was seeing a street, cobble-stoned and wet. It was raining. An old fashioned top hat fell upon the street and a horse-drawn carriage drove over the hat, smashing it in a puddle of water. I was that hat. Waking from the hallucination, I shouted, "Annette Long, what a bitch she was!" Now I was able to put a name to the little girl who had chased me. Then, fully aware and conscious with my friends, I told them about what I had seen and about the top hat that was me in my shame. Annette was just a little girl who didn't like me and had threatened me for some reason. It wasn't that I was afraid of her, it was just that I was taught that boys didn't hit girls. I ran from her and hid, not knowing what else to do. However, this shame had stayed buried within my mind from a very early age.

Another flash exploded into my mind.

Sitting on the floor in front of the fireplace with Marshall, I was rubbing my hands back and forth on the carpet and crying. "What are you doing?" Marshall asked.

"Rubbing my hands on the razor blades and pins," I sobbed. I could see the floor littered with sharp objects that were cutting my hands as I rubbed. Blood was flowing from the cuts onto the floor.

"Why don't you stop?" Marshall asked. "I can't," I replied.

I found myself following my father down the stairs into the basement. I was in my early teens. He acted as if there was a heavy weight upon his shoulders. He was shaking and his eyes were filled with tears.

Sitting on a wooden crate he sobbed, "If there is anything that I want before I die, it's for you to be proud of me." Then he put his head in his hands and cried.

I was not proud of my father. The fact was that I was ashamed of him. My father was an alcoholic who couldn't hold a job for very long. He seldom had money because he spent it on drinking with his friends. When he was drunk, the tightness would leave his facial muscles, causing his face to sag. He would talk with himself for hours before finally passing out.

I was in my mid teens when he found out I was gay; he would sit outside the open door to my bedroom and talk to himself about taking me to a whorehouse to "straighten" me out. He was a weak man in many ways, yet, he was loved by children and always carried candy in his pockets. He could fix a car, build things and paint. It was my father who taught me how to use tools. Because I was ashamed of him, I stayed away from Utah and my family. Finally, my father was committed to a hospital for acute alcoholism. When he came out of the hospital, he did quit drinking for a week or so, and then he died.

I could have been proud of him and showed him that proudness during the last few weeks of his life. Because I had stayed away, I did not know what had become of him. Now his words were booming within my head and I was lost within them. *"If there is anything that I want before I die, it's for you to be proud of me."*

"Mike, come back"!

Holding me and calling out to me, Jon was terrified. I had been in a coma for about a half hour. This memory had stayed hidden within my mind from a very early age. It was very painful for me to accept. I came back from the hallucination and told my friends what I had experienced. As I faced the vision and talked about it, the sadness eventually went away.

About that time I went to the bathroom and found myself looking into the mirror. My eyes found their own reflection and I was drawn through them into myself. The face in the mirror was beautiful, full of love and life. The lines of my face became as jewels and the image seemed like pictures I had seen of the blue Lord Krishna. However, as I looked deeper, the face changed and red jewels on the face turned into drops of blood. I saw a distorted and ugly thing staring back at me. Quickly, I turned and left the apparition behind. I wanted to be safe among my friends. Back in front of the fireplace, sitting on soft pillows, I finally relaxed.

Then I saw a large illuminated light expand from me, a six-pointed Star of David. I remembered the star-like flashes that had announced the other 'trips.' *If one tiny dot of light had announced such painful visions, what horror was this specter predicting for me?* The face appeared again between Marshall and myself. Lines in the face were crisp red, like rubies at first. Then the face became blue like the face I had seen of Krishna earlier. How very beautiful, loving and peaceful!

At that point, the rubies became drops of blood, running down his face. Blood ran down the walls, into the fireplace and across the floor. I screamed from the center of my being. I had to get away from that face which was drawing me in so deeply.

I could not allow myself to go into it so I ran from the house to the backyard. My friends came outside, but I screamed at them to stay away. Their very presence was triggering the vibrations. "Please leave me alone," I cried. Being outside and alone seemed to help a bit. My friends were very worried about me, and called a doctor friend of ours for help.

I was pacing back and forth to try to calm myself when I heard a gentle voice saying, "We have called the doctor. A prescription is on its way. Try to relax."

I had come to realize that by looking deeply into another's eyes, I would find "The Other Face." I did not realize it at that time, but the other face would then draw me deeply into journeys within myself.

Thorazine, a horse tranquilizer (I'm told) did, after a while, calm me down.

I remember that night lying in a strange place. My room, yet not my room. Time passing, yet not passing. Time had to pass. Would time never pass? Would I die before I awakened? Gritting my teeth, I longed for morning to come.

Daybreak came at last. I was still in a daze, floating somehow within my head. It was afternoon before I felt 'normal' again. "I will never take that stuff again," I swore. I was about 30 at that time and "bad" things pass away so I could never remember that I had said I wouldn't do it again until I was immersed in another trip. Yes, there would be others. Many of the trips that we took were fun and interesting; others were not. I would see something then become fixated on it until I was totally with it and experiencing what I was seeing. It was another place; sometimes it was hard and other times fun. I had learned that to begin a trip was to get entangled in it.

Although I didn't realize it at the time, the mood with which I would enter a trip would guide and permeate my experience.

Each time Marshall, myself, and a friend or two took a trip, I would make treats for us. Once I had made some Jell-O and wanting to spruce it up, I added some canned fruit. It was a cheap brand, but it was what I had on hand. When we got the munchies I served the salad. The fruit was tasteless and I said so. Rob, a gentle and good looking guy that I partnered with for several months was with us that night. "It's a gentle flavor but still very tasty,." he said. I took another taste and it was as if I was eating a ripe, freshly picked peach, warm from the sun; the taste was exquisite!

One time, I saw a giant smile which I floated toward. My body seemed to go through the smile and I remembered what a fun trip this was. Then I saw a giant frown which I went through as well, and I experienced a bad trip of some kind. "I've discovered the secret of acid," I exclaimed as I came back. "If you want to have a good trip, just keep going through the smiles." (Life is kind of like that.)

A month passed, *perhaps it was thirty days*.

"I have some window pane acid," Marshall said. "It's great!" Like a moth to a flame, I agreed to take it with him, not remembering the horrifying events that had taken place earlier. Nor, as I already stated, did I remember promising myself never to take acid again.

The evening came; candles, a fire in the fireplace, munchies and fruit. Clean body and again, a calm mind. Jon, my partner, joined us again. Jon rarely took an active part in our trips; mostly it was between Marshall and me. Jon told me later that he was always watching out for me. He was afraid that I would go too deep and get lost in a trip. Much of the time, Jon was in Chicago on business when we took LSD. Our paths were growing more and more apart. We were headed in different directions; he was becoming an executive for Sears Roebuck and Co. I was to become something totally different, although I didn't know it at the time.

Marshall and I settled onto the carpet in front of the fireplace and looked into each other's eyes. His reddish-blond curly hair was thick and reminded me of a wig of some kind. But his eyes called to me as I knew my eyes called to his. As I stated earlier, we had something between us, that something was honesty and that honesty created the "center face" that often appeared between us.

My trips always took me to places in my mind where I would go, experience something and then return. I knew the depths that this would lead me into and I was eager to follow.

One time I found myself looking at my hands. I was cupping something that was forming within them. Slowly, it grew into a hideous living mass of writhing repugnance. It was so repulsive that it seemed the very personification of ugliness and evil; yet, I felt that I could not reject this vile mass. Somehow, I had to make myself love this apparition. *"If I can love this thing,"* I thought, *"I can love all things."* Commanding tremendous amounts of inner strength, I forced myself to kiss this mass which represented to me perhaps the source of evil itself. With my kiss, the vision disappeared.

The light began to dim and it grew darker; like a giant curtain was coming down. Everything I could see was slowly being blackened out. It was as if a universal eye were closing upon all of creation, cutting off light into a darkness deeper than any I have ever known. After that, a slice of light appeared in the darkness which widened slowly, allowing more light to shine as if the giant eye was opening again. I thought of this as being the blinking of God's eye.

Looking up, I saw a well-dressed man sitting on my couch with his legs crossed. Everything was normal about him except that where his head should have been was a brightly shining ball of light. I knew that he was watching to see what I was going to do.

Again, my visual perceptions changed. Everything that I was looking at seemed to be growing outward from itself and manifesting in a myriad of different ways with the expansion. The visions of this place and time were becoming entangled with succeeding moments that were extending outward and unfolding as here and now grew from, and into, a timeless totality of Its Self.

I was seeing past the ordinary three dimensions and experiencing 'now' as it progressed into the depth that is time itself. To me, it looked like a mass of writhing worms. From this I learned that we travel through a content of being-ness and call it time.

Time is not linear; time IS.

I did not think more of the man on the couch nor of the evil mass nor of my vision of time because another flash of light shaped like a large six-pointed star burst into my vision.

I found myself "journeying outward." In the background, I could feel blood. I could see blood coming from the fireplace, from the walls and from Marshall's eyes.

Eyes, always it was the eyes. Looking into eyes became pathways into the soul and a trap to lock me into the coming trip. Once I looked into them, they were magnetic; difficult to look away from and drawing me deeper. Now they were drawing me into the blood.

Shaking with fear and with a feeling of impending doom, I ran from the house. Jon and Marshall ran after me to help, but what had begun with the eyes, was amplified by their very closeness. Now their own personal energy was triggering the visions to become stronger.

I begged them to call the doctor and get help—to go away and leave me alone. "This is why I didn't want to take acid again," I yelled. Again, they had a prescription of Thorazine delivered to the house.

"Never again," I vowed. "I have learned my lesson and will not do it again—period." But, of course, I did.

Our trips together had sort of a pattern to them. Soon after taking the pill, we would feel the effects of the acid coming on. I would feel paranoid for a time; then soon I would see paisley patterns growing from lines around faces. Getting lost in the patterns, I would experience different and wonderful things. Afterwards I would experience blood and fear. Always blood accompanied by unbelievable fear. I would run from the house and they would have to get Thorazine to bring me back down. We called it my "blood trip."

Marshall was always there for me. Many times, he gave up the enjoyment of his own trip to help me when I found myself out of control and frightened.

Some times I wonder why Marshal kept bringing the acid when it always ended up with me needing attention from everyone else.

I would go off into unknown regions where my perceptions of reality changed. I got lost in my trips while he was just enjoying the patterns.

I conceived of the idea that I might be seeing sound and hearing sight, that my senses had been cross-wired somehow. (In the film *What the bleep do we know,* scientists explain that this is indeed so). I felt that this cross-wiring was allowing my mind to bypass blinders to my own perceptions, blinders that I had put in place over many years.

As I ventured behind the blinders of my mind, I discovered numerous things from the past that I had buried deeply within myself. As I talked about these situations, I became liberated from them. Once this occurred, I was able to see more clearly. Confession, they say, is good for the soul.

Jon had moved to Chicago by this time and I was alone in the house. I began to frequent a fun bar called The Klondike. It had a player piano around which we would gather and sing as we ate our 10 cent (later 25 cent) lunches. One day, I was sitting at the bar looking at a life-sized picture of a handsome go-go dancer on the stage. I turned to the guy sitting next to me. "I sure would like to meet him," I said. He looked at me and replied, "You're sitting next to him." Thus, I met Buddy. We liked each other immediately and became very close friends; he even moved in with me for a time. Buddy was putting together a pantomime show for the bar. However, a week or so before the opening, Buddy's partner quit.

"You're on," Buddy seemed to be saying as he quickly began setting up skits for me to do. I had not been the first choice to be co-actor, but I was all he had. I wasn't all that sure that I would be very good at performing, but once on stage, it was as if I came alive. I began to love acting and the audience began to love me. We performed in the bar for 18 weeks. We called it "The Buddy and Mike Show."

Shortly thereafter, I began to feel weak, and my eyes turned yellow. When the doctor told me that I had hepatitis, he also said that I could not exert myself at all and had to have someone take care of me. I wasn't sure how I could do that because I was living alone at the time. I asked him what would happen if I took care of myself. "Then you'll die," the doctor answered and moved on to see the next patient.

My friend Buddy took me in and lovingly nursed me back to health.

Buddy also helped me to understand that there is another more mystical side to life. He helped me to comprehend that there was much more to me than I had believed myself to be. He taught me to read *The New Tarot for the Aquarian Age*, a New Tarot deck that had just been released. Aside from the Tarot readings, he also gave me readings, that came through him from his spiritual guide whose name was Vivian. They were surprisingly accurate. Buddy was a trance medium.

When I recovered from hepatitis, Buddy and I decided to take LSD together. We were in my room after taking the acid. All of a sudden, he looked at me in horror. He was shaking as he shrunk back into the corner, crouched down and cried, "You're God!" He would not let me approach him. In the terror of what he was seeing in me, he was quickly losing control of himself. In desperation I said, "Of course I am. Now calm down," or something of that nature. It took a while. However Buddy did calm down and we continued to share a trip together.

For some reason, I could never remember the terrible fears I faced while on LSD. "Bad trips," people called them. For the most part, people took acid and went out to party in bars or with friends. They would play with the colors and the changed perceptions. I went inside of myself and confronted my hidden memories and hidden demons.

One day, Marshall told me that he had some acid mixed with speed. "It's great," he said. Without any consideration for my earlier resolution never to take acid again, I leaped at the chance to take another trip. "Is tonight too soon?" Before I knew it, I was setting up my house: fruits and sweet things, fruit juice to drink, a warm fire, and just the right records to play. *Can I handle the music of Ravi Shankar tonight?*

When Marshall arrived, I was getting into comfortable clothes in my bedroom. I could remember some of the things that had happened on prior trips, but not the feelings that caused me to scream for Thorazine and rush from the house. I felt that I could handle whatever came up for me that night.

"Do you love me?" I asked Marshall and Rob. Rob was another friend who had joined us that evening. They must have responded in a positive manner because I responded, "Then I give you me." I did not know what was to confront me but I was determined not to hold back from whatever came. I wanted to give my all to these people who had loved and stood by me.

I was sitting in a lotus position watching the lines on Marshall's face as they became beautiful paisley patterns in vivid colors. I was beguiled by the patterns and lost in my thoughts. Then there seemed to be a "blinking"—I just went away for a moment. When I came back I could remember living an entire lifetime in the moment that had just passed. I remembered events in that life, and even the death that was not a death but an "awakening," to find myself back with my friends again. It was as if a moment of my life had expanded to include a totally different life.

Realizing what had just passed, I was terrified that I had

been caught up in some kind of "controlling" life: living lives one after another within itself, then dying only to return to the fireplace and my friends. I had an intense fear that I would die of old age before the effects of the acid could wear off.

Then, I suddenly felt that time itself was speeding up. Faster and faster, it seemed, as if I could see this moment passing by me in waves of here and now. Although my body was still, it seemed to be speeding through a mass of time itself. Time lightninged through the cosmos of my mind like memories of a storm just passed. Faster and faster it went. "Now" was passing by before I had a chance to experience it. I could also feel the past rushing away behind me. I felt that I could not sustain this great speed and knew that I had to stop myself somehow. With all of my might, I pushed down within myself. The only way I can describe it is as if I were putting brakes on like in a car, slamming myself to a stop.

At that point, it seemed time sped past me leaving blurred line patterns behind it. The effect was of everything around me, rushing forward pulling me with it while I was pulling back. I was being stretched out. The front of my body seemed to keep going with the speeding time. The skin of my face stretched out like an elongated balloon etched with my facial features. My eyeballs extruded from my head, lengthening a foot or more out from my extended face. Then from the pupils of my eyes, mouths extended which then opened in stretched agony to reveal tongues also reaching out, then splaying apart.

I felt that I was about to lose my mind; this was more than I could handle. I simply could not contain this experience. Then I remembered seeing a Peter Max painting of something similar and it gave me the strength I needed to control my mind. *If Peter Max has seen something like this and survived to paint it, I can handle it as well,* I thought.

Then time stopped. It was no longer passing me by but had stopped as abruptly as it had sped by. Time itself had stopped still. I looked at the clock. The second hand did not move. No matter how long I stared at the clock I could not look long enough for the second hand to move. Time, for me, was standing still. Again I was terrified that I would die of old age before the effects of the pill wore off.

Then there was blood.

Blood was flowing from the chimney. I saw blood flowing from Marshall's eyes.

Three, fiery six-pointed stars appeared in a row in front of my vision, glowing outward from their own centers and forming themselves. I did not have the courage to face what it was that this specter was predicting for me. I knew that I could not face this trip. I told my friends about the three blazing stars I had seen and how frightened I was of them.

Marshall asked me if I wanted to take the trip or if I wanted to "close the window" on it. I finally told him that I needed to "close the window." I could not face what was to come. He gave me a piece of candy to help me relax. As I took a bite of the candy it was as if every tooth in my head was suddenly crunched out and I was chewing upon my own teeth. I knew that I needed to go through whatever this vision was foretelling.

I saw myself lying in the swing in the back of the house. I was in my early teens. I had picked my nose and was about to dispose of it the easiest way, by eating it. "Michael!" I heard my Father yell. "Stop that, it's sickening!" My Dad had been watching me from the house to see what I did when I thought I was alone. I then saw "the middle face" between Marshall and myself touch its nose, then touch its mouth.

"I pick my nose and eat it," I said. Shock pasted the faces of my friends. It was as if I had slapped them. I felt naked, unprotected and totally defenseless, all I could say was, "But I don't do it any more." And in that moment, a habit that had been with me all of my life was taken away.

Then I saw the inside of my head. It appeared as a smooth, seamless, stainless steel container. I had confessed everything there was for me to confess. My mind was clear. There were no more cobwebs inside of me. The blood was the deepest secret that I had left to tell. No wonder, each time, I had run from its truth.

I was free now, freer than I had ever been before. There were no secrets left to hide. And I realized that secrets that we hold become blinders in front of our vision and limiters to our lives.

Now I was clean, and I knew the meaning of real truth. I have seldom found a need to tell a lie since that time. When the deepest secrets are uncovered there is no more need for small lies.

Slowly at first, then faster, it began to get lighter; brightness surrounded everything and grew so intense I could hardly bear to watch. Light was surrounding me as well, and drawing me downward somehow. It was like I was on a flag pole of infinite length, greased and slippery. I was sliding down the pole, faster and faster into the light; I was becoming the light. Then I stopped sliding and found myself standing in my kitchen. It was like I was on Mount Olympus of the ancient Gods. I was just in my kitchen, but now it was more. It was... Holy.

As I stood there, I felt as if all of time and space came from this Holy place. There was a "life—ness" about everything and I knew that this was a place of God.

I could see and hear a bird singing in a tree full of blossoms outside the window. A blue sky with beautiful clouds expressed eternal spring—It had been raining when we began the trip, and there was no tree outside of the window.

I had just finished cleansing myself. With this cleansing I was able to see and experience past the normal three dimensions into a vastness that contained time itself.

Suddenly I knew that everything and all of us are God, and that we are all Holy and in a Holy place. God is not somewhere out there and separate but here, now, and personal.

There was no way that I could contain this knowledge by myself. I had never heard or thought of God in this manner. God had always been a man on a throne somewhere in heaven. *Not here and not now, not you and certainly not me.* I could not handle being the only one on earth to know what I knew then. This was more than I could handle alone.

"Marshall," I screamed, "we're God!"

"Jesus Christ," Marshall replied. "Are you just learning that?" He made me feel like an infant just learning something new. I was fine as long as someone else knew. In the morning, I told Marshall about how he had saved my sanity by his simple statement. He did not remember saying it, and in describing to him what I had seen, I realized that he had no idea of what I was talking about. The "Other image" between Marshall and myself had saved my sanity.

Somehow I made it through the following days and weeks. The vastness of what I had encountered pushed against the limits of my ability to grasp. My mind was bursting and I was overwhelmed. I could not contain its totality within my brain. I could neither see a reason to live nor a reason to die. I was aimless, and I was facing what to me was a terrible choice: I was either going to have to give up the Mormon Church and the God that I had come to believe in through that church, or I was going to have to deny my own experience.

The Mormon Church teaches of a hell deeper than hell for those who leave "The Church." It is called "The Sons of Perdition" and I did not want to go there. And yet, what I had actually seen was so much more than what I had learned in church. I simply could not deny my experience.

Then I prayed, really prayed, probably for the first time in my life. I was crying deeply from my heart when inside of my head I heard a woman's voice. "Oh, don't worry," she said. "You don't have to leave the church. Just grow beyond it." I was shown a vision of many people worshiping in various ways. I was shown Jews in their Synagogues, Mormons in their Temples, Muslims in their Mosques and American Indians around a Medicine Circle. I was shown many others—and they were all acceptable. I understood that it doesn't matter what you believe. What matters is what you do with what you believe. Hypocrisy is the error, not the belief.

Jesus of Nazareth is quoted as saying that the truth shall set you free. It had taken my blood to do it, but I had confessed the whole truth, and now I was indeed, free.

And so I came to accept what I had begun to comprehend. I had grown up with a vision of God being a man on a throne as I am sure, many people have. Yet, as I write this years later, I remember there were clues for those who looked: As a young Mormon boy (a Deacon), when I read the prayer for the sacrament, there was a phrase, "And witness unto Thee, oh God, the Eternal Father, that they do take upon themselves, the name of Thy Son." There is also a saying often quoted in the church and I had said it myself, "As man is, God once was, as God is man may become." So what I had seen did not really conflict with these teachings hidden in plain view among the rituals of the church.

I tried to tell people what I had seen. I was so excited. I tried to tell them that we are all God and that this realization lay hidden behind the blinders of our own secrets. One day as I was telling a friend of my new-found knowledge she said, "Mike, we just don't want to hear that." As my brother said, "Those who have ears let them hear. Those who have eyes let them see." We all see with different eyes. This too, I had learned, although I was not to realize it for several decades.

Each of us has our own pathway that we must walk. God—(that which is more than one can comprehend) is seen and experienced by each person differently. No two people can see the same thing from the same perspective even if you stand next to one another, and no two people can see the same God; it simply cannot be done.

I had a dream during this time. In the dream I was a soldier reporting back to a Sergeant in heaven. The Sergeant was reprimanding me for being late. I was imploring him to show mercy, saying, "But Sir, have you never been born in," and I pointed to a map that had appeared with the state of Utah highlighted.

Not long after this time, I became a hippie. Dissatisfied with the person that I had been up to that point, I gave all of my belongings away: my home, my car and my money. I quit my job, my career and the life that I had created, behind.

At one point, I found myself surrounded by a younger crowd. They had taken acid, smoked pot and participated in whatever the younger people did during those days; therefore, they were much more receptive to me and they loved hearing my stories. One day, I was telling the story about my "blood trip" to a young man. When I finished, he said to me, "I pick my nose and eat it."

I thought about the pain that I had experienced; the fear that I had to master, and the great price that I had paid to be able to make that simple statement.

"That's my trip," I said. "You'll have to find your own." I read somewhere that if we all confessed our "sins," we would be amazed by our lack of originality.

Note: In reality, I took about 12 or more LSD trips, always with my friend Marshall; sometimes with others as well. They were taken at my home in Silverlake, California, covering a period of more than a year during 1969 and 1971.

Chapter 2

Meeting the Hippies

T he blacksmith heats the metal. When the metal has reached the correct temperature, the blacksmith begins to form the metal into the desired shape. For me, the heating of the metal came with the trips that I took on acid. The forming of the metal began when I met the Hippies.

MF/BB 29

I was building furniture in my garage. That was the way I relaxed after a day of programming. Something about working with wood "worked" and still works for me. Designing, then creating with my own hands, relieved me of the tedium of my job and my life. As it turned out, I was one of the first computer programmers in the world.

The afternoon was upon me. Someone was walking up my driveway; a long-haired, barefooted hippie freak! How could this be? I lived in a respectable neighborhood, even upscale. My two-story house was on a slight hill that overlooked Silverlake reservoir in Los Angeles.

You have the wrong person. You are not at the right place. Why are you coming here? My mind was reeling. What if someone were to see? Dirty, shoeless, with long unkempt hair and a HIPPIE!

I brushed the sawdust off of me. As he came closer, I realized that I knew the face. Good God! It was John, John Chess. *John with the good job.* Now to see him in this state. I wondered what could have happened to him? Drugs—It had to be drugs that has brought him so low. He was coming to see me! *Does he want money?* Embarrassed, I turned away, brushing more sawdust out of my hair. "*What does he want from me?*" I thought. I worked as he watched and commented. I tried not to sound overly interested or to say anything that might start an actual conversation. I just wanted him to go away and not embarrass me.

The night was drawing closer. Coffee! That magic drink that turns evening into a darkened daylight. If he would leave, I could have a cup. By habit, I asked, "You want a cup of coffee?" (I was praying that he wouldn't but, of course, he did). "I'll get us some and be right back," I told him and turned to go inside.

He's following me! I don't want him inside
    — to see
        and to know—
           Me.

My big house was showy, with expensive furniture, velvet drapes and original oil paintings on the walls.
I'm a success, don't you see?

"You don't have a dining room set," John said as he entered my velvet-draped dining room. My one-of-a-kind chandelier was hanging over the spot where the dining table used to be. The question made me feel very uncomfortable. Why would he have to pick the very thing I lacked instead of commenting on the velvet drapes and paintings?

"Jon and I broke up. He took the dining room set as part of our separation agreement," I told him as I headed for the kitchen. I was, of course, embarrassed that he had seen the empty space.

"You need a dining room set and I have one I'll give to you," he said. In my mind, I pictured a spindly, cheap, white-painted table with two equally cheap chairs. Good for the poor in their small apartments but not for my formal dining room. "No thanks," I replied, "I have. . . plans."

"No, I insist. Let's get the table and we'll have our coffee on it," John exclaimed. "It's right around the corner and we can use your truck to carry it. Come on, it will only take a moment." John would not take no for an answer. Finally, just to get him to leave, I agreed. We drove down the block to a run-down house not too far away, just down the hill.

He knocked on the door and shouted inside, "Hey, it's John. I've come for the table and chairs." From inside, I heard a woman's voice. "Thank God. I thought you'd never get it out of here." Naturally, I was far from overjoyed to hear that reply.

John pulled old clothes, odd pieces of furniture and toys off of a huge pile of what looked like junk. "Here it is," he said, pulling away an old blanket. As he worked to free the set, he pulled out a huge black object. I couldn't see what it was until he sat it on the floor. It was a leather, overstuffed swivel chair with armrests, balanced on chrome legs with rollers. It was beautiful! John pulled three more chairs from the pile, which then uncovered the table. It was four feet round, solid walnut, edged in the same chrome as the chairs. The set was magnificent; it could have fit nicely in any executive suite and would, indeed, fit very well with my velvet drapes and my one-of-a-kind chandelier.

Back at my house, with the dining room now complete, we had our coffee. And to think I had not wanted to have coffee with this man! I should have been grateful. However, the feeling I really had was that I still wanted him to go. He wasn't as dirty as I had originally thought, but he did have long hair and bare feet. It was obvious that he was a hippie and I wasn't anxious for anyone to think that I, a programmer and an executive, would be associating with a hippie!

Coffee finished, I wanted to go back to building my furniture. "I'm having some friends over for dinner tonight," he said. "I'd like you to join us." *Not on your life,* I thought, and made a weak excuse.

John persisted and I finally realized that with his gift, which easily would have cost a fortune, I did at least owe him the courtesy of dropping by. This was, however, the last thing I wanted to do.

The address that John gave me led to a run-down section of town. On the side of a steep hill, small pairs of dilapidated looking units (small two-room houses) paired their way up with wooden stairs climbing in between them. There were dirty children playing and people with rags around their heads, sweatbands, I think they called them. Everything seemed unkempt; the children, the small houses, the people, the grounds, everything. I really did not want to see it nor to be there.

I found the small house about two-thirds of the way up the stairs. Taking a deep breath, I knocked on the door which was immediately opened. I could not see the person who had opened the door but I did see a mass of people, all of whom seemed scruffy and dirty.

The house was packed. Each person looked more ominous

and unwashed than the next. I had no intention of pushing my way into the house and turned to go. "Michael" rang out loudly above the din. "Come in and go into the front room. I'll join you in a minute." I could see John standing on a chair, stirring a huge pot of something on the stove.

I was caught. There was little I could politely do to extricate myself from what I envisioned as a very bad situation. Being polite was very important to me; more important than owning my own feelings, I think. Slowly, I edged my way through the kitchen toward the other room. There were so many people that I could barely move at all. Squeezing into what seemed to be the front room, I stood flush against the wall, fervently hoping that no one would touch me. I had never seen so many people packed together in my life. As I stood against the wall, I became claustrophobic. I knew I was going to have to leave when I noticed a space in the middle of the room. It was a place where there were no people. *A coffee table!* Desperately, I thought if I could go and stand on it, I'd have some room.

I slowly made my way to the center of the room. Easing myself through the crowd toward the table, I squeezed between two people who were standing in my way and began to step onto what I thought was the coffee table. As I took the step, I noticed that it was not a table at all, but a group of six or eight people sitting in a circle around a candle on the floor. As I leaned in, they noticed me. As one, they moved to make room for me to join them.

"Who ARE these people?" I asked as I sat down. One of the seated hippies answered, "They're just low riders. Welcome, Brother." Someone passed a joint around the circle and we all smoked. After that, someone passed a glass of water and we all drank from the same cup; they called it, "Sharing water."

And that's how I met the hippies.

The evening somehow progressed. I do not remember the "low riders" leaving and I do not remember John joining the circle, but from the moment I met the hippies, I entered into a parallel universe; apart, yet not apart from the surroundings that I had been used to. I am still in that space and time. Sometimes it resembles the place where most people live, and sometimes it's a world quite apart.

From that eventful day on, I spent almost every night with them. I never did go back to John's place but we all got together at a house that Mary, one of the hippie ladies, shared with several others.

How did I go from that very afternoon wanting John to just go away to spending every night with him and the others? I was as ripe as a plum about to drop from a tree of its own accord.

This period of time had been pointed out several years earlier by my friend, John Keel, an avid and competent astrologer. Pointing to what he called a "grand trine" consisting of the Sun, Moon and Neptune in my chart. He noted that sometime around the age of 30, my ruling planet Saturn would be completing its orbit around the sun. Saturn, the teaching planet, would be finishing one lesson and beginning another cycle of learning and growth for me. At the same time, John continued, Saturn's return would affect the grand trine and I could expect momentous changes in my life. When I asked him what he thought would happen, he answered that I would probably start my own religion. It would seem that with this series I have done just that.

As I made friends with the hippies, I didn't connect what was happening in my life to the prediction John had made. I knew that the coming "Age of Aquarius" was being embraced by hippies and spiritual people around the world. What I didn't think of however, was that my own stars were drawing me into an entirely new life.

"It's all over, over 30," went the chant. I was 31 and determined not to be left behind. I grabbed the Aquarian age like it was a train leaving the station. As John had been predicted, this was going to be the ultimate life change for me, I was never to be the same again.

I had left my home in Utah and moved to California when I was 19 in order to be with people "of my own kind." Also because my family were Mormons from farm stock and simply would not be able to understand the person that I was.

It wasn't long before I began work as a messenger from the tabulating department at Technicolor Motion Picture Corporation in Hollywood. Within a few months I was singled out to be trained as a computer programmer—the field was just opening up at that time. The company did not know how to classify programmers; we certainly were not clerks, nor were we executives. They ended up lumping us into the higher group. Thus it was that at 20, with barely any work experience, I ended up classed as an executive, working at a high paying and respected job.

Over the ensuing years, I had created a life for myself that included several different relationships; a lot of friends, always a good job, a home, car, money and lots of showy possessions. Soon I was to leave that life behind. The hippies helped me through the change. I did not know it at the time, but within a few months I was to leave the hippies behind as well.

Fool that I was, I decided to throw a large party to introduce my old friends to these new friends of mine. I was very naive to have thought it would work. The evening was to drive the final wedge from one life to the other for me. As my old friends came into my house they saw my new hippie friends and were appalled; appalled as I had been at first.

One of the hippies brought out a joint which he offered around. I did take a hit but my old group of friends, recoiling in horror, did not. Needless to say, the two groups did not blend at all. Soon after the party most of my old friends simply faded away. After all the years we had spent together as friends, they had become a habit in my life as I had become in theirs. Marshall actively remained my friend as did my best friend,

Little Mike. Both were to play major roles in my new lives to come.

The life I had been living revolved around a secure and well-paying job, expensive possessions, comfort, lots of friends, game nights and plays or movies. There were plenty of arguments one way or another, and we had to watch out for someone cheating at cards; *I know I occasionally cheated.* Words had to be weighed as well, for little lies made their way into our conversations at times, just to add some zest to the discussions, but lies just the same.

What a different way of life I was to find as I grew closer to the hippies. They lived lives that grew outward from love and truth; simple lives that didn't depend upon possessions as status symbols.

While I enjoyed being with them, I kept living my own life much the same as I had before meeting John. I was comfortable in my life and saw no reason to change it.

When I was with the hippies we laid on the floor with pillows or sat on saggy couches and shared water, joints and trips. Other than the trips on LSD I really hadn't smoked much pot, but when I was with them we usually got buzzed.

Probably because of my recent experiences with LSD, I would get very high when I smoked pot and go places in my mind not dis-similar to some of the acid trips.

Gently, the hippies encouraged me to tell them what I was experiencing. They understood and guided me with love. Their support encouraged me, which in turn gave me the strength I needed to face the strange and often scary world that I was seeing. They taught me many things about the nature of what I had experienced and in turn they let me teach them as well. In this way their very presence began changing my life. Through talking about the ideas and visions I was experiencing, I began learning about what is called, "Multidimensional reality," and about the vision that I had called God.

One night I felt myself growing outward. Out and out I went.

Growing bigger, expanding out into the cosmos. I could feel and see entire universes within me and I was terrified. "I'm growing bigger and bigger and I can't stop," I cried. John began to shake; he was caught up with what I was saying and was afraid as well. Finally, I could stand no more. Somehow I managed to turn my focus from looking outward to looking within.

There in the black void that surrounded me, I saw a spot so small as only infinites could see, and I knew that spot was me. The pressure from outside then started to squeeze my awareness until I was so compressed that I became that spot, with the entire universe crushing down and compressing me into nothingness. Something had to change.

I caused myself to look outward again. The immense pressure was still pushing against me. Desperately I took a deep breath and forced it to grow inside of me. Slowly, with each breath, I began to expand again. As I felt myself increase in size, I could see my image growing and stretching balloon-like within my awareness. I could feel my eyes enlarging into huge spheres as the image grew, and I felt that I could see everything, as what I was seeing became all inclusive. Then I felt myself "snap" into what I imagined was a "balancing" or "center place" with equal parts inside and equal parts outside, the image of myself being the dividing line.

Before long I was again in my body and calm returned. I felt that I had experienced what is referred to as the Yin/Yang symbol.

My hippie friends taught me that, "We are One." I had heard the phrase before but actions speak much louder than words. A group of us were all together and someone passed a cigarette around as we would have done with pot. At these times, cigarettes were used everywhere. I even smoked cigarettes, a lot. As the cigarette made its way around the circle, Mary who didn't smoke, took a puff and coughed. John, I think it was, apologized to Mary, telling her that he had envisioned her taking the puff.

John, Mary and Beautiful James were the ones to whom I grew closest. We all called James, Beautiful James, probably because his face always radiated innocence and peace, and light seemed to shine from him. They called me Michael. I had always insisted on being called Mike but when they said Michael, I heard for the first time the gentleness and love associated with the name. Since that time, I prefer to be called Michael: the name fits me more now.

There was a time when John and Beautiful James were with me in my home. We were standing in the upstairs hallway just outside of my bedroom. John was saying, "Michael, do you understand what James is saying to you? He is saying that he will make love with you if you want." This was indeed, a time of free love; James was straight, or at least I thought he was, and I surmised that this would be too much for him to give. So I said, "No, it is not necessary," as my own gift in return.

They really were "Love children," these hippies. The simple honesty, true caring and giving that we shared taught me something, something that I had sorely needed in my life.

- - The hippies taught me to love.

Although I could not have known it at the time, when the long-haired hippie walked up my driveway, my life would change dramatically; though I myself had to be almost dragged into their midst to actually "see" them.

The visions I had, along with the guidance from my new friends, and the alignment of the stars themselves, were pulling upon me. As had been predicted years earlier, I had to change; there was no other way. How to change was the question now.

I got together again with Marshall during that time. I wanted him to enjoy an acid trip with me where I didn't run out of the house and ruin his trip. So I made everything comfortable and warm. We took the pills. At first, everything felt just fine. Soon however, I was filled with apprehension and fear. I really didn't want to let Marshall know what was happening with me so I called John and Mary. It was not long before five or six of my hippie friends were with us, just blending in. John told me that he could feel our energy as soon as they turned the corner leading to my house.

Time passed and seasons change. Christmas was coming. I had always gone "home" to Utah, That place that kept drawing me back was calling to me again. "I have no place to go, can I go to Utah with you?" John asked.

Totally forgetting the horror that my old friends had felt when meeting the hippies, I blithely called my sister and asked if I could bring John. As I described him I fantasized that I could have been describing Jesus; "Long hair, gentle and giving, full of love." Of course I was also describing a hippie. While I had come to accept hippies, most other people had not. "Please don't bring your friend," she said. "Christmas should only be for the family."

How many people had I turned away simply because they were different or how they looked? Certainly, I had tried to do so when I saw the long-haired hippie walking up my driveway not so long ago. Even now I am not "all accepting." I know my life would be so much richer if I could get rid of personal judgment. This is neither good or bad. However, each person we turn away is an experience we don't get to enjoy, and a new way that we don't get to grow.

I made a Christmas card that year: Although I've now made a "Season card" every year for over a quarter of a century, this first card was the only time I referred to Christmas in my cards. Even then I did not write the word.

> Xmas is love for the whole -
>> family.
>
> Xmas is a gift that you got last year. You'd like to give it away
>> but you can't remember who gave it to you, so you won't.
>
> Xmas is hanging the tinsel on the tree with joy and singing
>> but the night ending in arguments.
>
> Xmas is a big gift for Uncle Joe; he gave you a big gift last year,
>> and a small one for Aunt Em because hers was little.
>
> Xmas is going to church
>> but you have to call to find out what time it starts.
>
> Xmas is trying to do in one day, with one gift,
>> the things you've been meaning to do all year.
>
> Xmas is looking at a strange reflection of yourself
>> in the balls on the tree.
>
> Xmas is "Over again for another year.
>> Thank God!"
>
> When will they learn that Xmas starts with a "C"?

After receiving my card, my aunt Amy sent me a letter saying that she was reading my card and trying not to be a hypocrite. Funny, she was the only one I could think of that I'd have believed to be honestly herself.

My comfortable life

Good job

Nice house

Building furniture for fun

All of this is about to change

Chapter 3

Move a Mountain and Give a House Away

Mind expanding drugs had set the stage for experiences beyond the normal, and my wonderful friends, the hippies, had helped me to make some sense of these experiences.

Stability in my life was being eroded; Jon was gone, my long-time friends were mostly gone and even my comfortable ways of thinking were being altered.

The only thing left was to change myself.

My home seemed empty. Jon was gone now, working in Chicago. Most of my friends, good friends that I had had for years, faded away after the party. As I spent more time with my new hippie brothers and sisters, I happened upon a guy of my own age who was looking for a place to live. He seemed like a nice guy so I decided to rent a room to him. I had a truck and enjoyed lending a hand to other people, so I helped him to move in. This surprised him because we didn't even know each other yet.

We had just moved everything of his into the house when he got a phone call. His father in New York had had a heart attack. He hadn't even been able to unpack and he was going to have to move to New York with the realization that he had just found a friend. Packing the things he would take to New York, he began placing things aside that would have to be left behind; some of which I would ship to him later, some he just gave to me. He gave me a huge reel-to-reel tape recorder, (very impressive for its day) and two huge and imposing speakers. There was a pile of clothes, with several Bell bottom pants, the latest fashion. He gave me these things to lighten his load.

When he had finished packing and was about to leave, I realized how very much he had given to me and how much trust he had for me, a stranger until just a few days earlier.

I wanted to give him a gift in return so I went upstairs to my bedroom where I grabbed the first thing that caught my eye: a beautiful, gold travel clock with naked Roman athletes tooled in black around the side. A perfect gift! I was heading back downstairs when I realized that this clock was one of a limited edition of only 50 that had been made to commemorate the Japan Olympics. I couldn't give THAT away! I took it back to my room and exchanged it for a small painting of a strawberry. I was going back down the stairs when I realized that the painting had been a birthday gift, painted by a friend. How could I give THAT away? So I took that back into my room as well. I looked about for something else to give, but for some reason everything else just looked cheap.

I thought of going back without a gift, but he had given me so much. So I took a small glazed jar that really wasn't very good and headed back downstairs. As I walked down the stairs, the walls seemed to close in on me; the ceiling which was slanted to align with the stairs, lowered to block me, and the stairwell narrowed as if it didn't want me to pass.

Standing at the top of the stairs, I came face-to-face with my own addiction to possessions. I did not possess my possessions; my possessions possessed me! I hurried back to my room and took the little golden travel clock from the shelf. It was the perfect gift to give. Giving the clock to my new friend seemed to open a floodgate within me. I wanted to give. Within six months I was to give my house, my truck, my money and all of my possessions away. I would quit my job and become a free spirit; a love child, a hippie.

If you walked down Wilshire Boulevard in Los Angeles, you could easily see my office. Every window in the Gibraltar Savings & Loan building had blinds drawn against the sun. Except for one window somewhere in the middle of the eighth floor, my office and my window. I used to sit in the window to do my programming. I loved the sun and I could never understand why everyone else closed their blinds to it. I had said that I would never work for a bank but here I was, doing just what I had said I would never do.

A year earlier I had received a call from what we called a "head hunter." He worked for an employment agency and said that he had a job for me, at a bank. "No thanks," I said. "I don't want to work for a bank," and I hung up. A few days later I got another call from him, "They really want you," he told me. I repeated that I still did not want to work for a bank and hung up again. Yet another day and another call. "What time do you go to work?" The head hunter asked.

"Seven AM," I replied.

"The vice-president of Gibraltar Savings and Loan, Computer Division, will meet you at his office tomorrow at 6:30

AM if you will agree to come," He told me. I decided that if a vice president would come in at that hour just to meet with me, I should at least hear what he had to say.

I stood, leaning on the door frame and he looked up. "I don't want to work for you," I told him.

"I know," he replied.

Still standing at the doorway, I said, "I won't cut my hair." It was shoulder length, an affectation of the times.

"You will be the only one in the bank with long hair, but I accept," he told me.

"I won't shave my mustache." (Hair seemed to be the in-thing in the 60s.) "Everyone else is clean shaven, but it's also okay," he said. I told him that I wouldn't wear dress clothes I wanted to wear Levis and a T-shirt. He told me that since I would not be working on the banking floor, it would be acceptable. I also wanted to work early in the morning; I was rising well before the sun at that time, and I found that I could make my own hours. I refused to remove my earring. An earring and long hair were considered "freak flags" and I was proud of them—also accepted. After a while, I had run out of the things that I wouldn't do. He had agreed to everything that I wanted and I could see no reason why I shouldn't accept the job.

Now, a year later, after taking several acid trips, I had seen a vision that I called God. Being with my hippie friends showed me a reflection of myself that I did not like, and increasingly I wanted to change who and what I was.

I had been swept up in the feeling of the '60s and '70s. There was a new world coming and I wanted to be a part of it.

I continued to do my programming but I had become increasingly restless. I was aimless at work. My mind was not on programming. I had not been able to concentrate on programming for several weeks as the visions that I had had on the acid trips continued to pound against the boundaries of my mind. I realize now that I was trying to make sense of other dimensions that had shoved themselves into my three-dimensional brain and it just wasn't working.

More and more I would write a line or so of code then go for walks down quiet alleyways to see if I could clear the pressure that was building up within my head. Short aphorisms and sayings began to come unbidden to my mind, repeatedly crowding out any attempt at programming. Often I wrote the sayings down instead..

> *It is good to speak to the mountain,*
> *for you cannot say, "You lie," to an echo.*

> *First you must pour of your wine;*
> *only then will your cup be filled.*

> *Eat sometimes of a lemon, that you might know*
> *the sweetness of your own mouth.*

> *I am no less than the greatest,*
> *nor greater than the least.*

> *In every hell is a bit of heaven,*
> *and therein lies our salvation.*
> *In every heaven is a bit of hell,*
> *and therein lies our growth.*

The sayings just kept coming into my head. I wrote them down on small pieces of paper and pasted them in random fashion all over my desk and office. My office was referred to as *Poor Richard's almanac*. Each day, people would come by to see what was newly written on my walls. Eventually, I collected them into a book called, *Me, My Brother and I*.

I was still very troubled by the tightness within my brain and I tried to forget what I had seen and experienced, but the memories would not let go of me. The knowledge was like a growing thing pushing against my mind. I tried to digest this knowledge, but it was too much for me. I felt that I was slowly growing insane; to me, a fate worse than death. (I do understand, now, why those who have "seen" say it cannot be explained with words.) One day I heard someone mention the phrase, Universal Mind. This is a phrase used by several New Age spiritual groups.

A Universal Mind, I thought, could contain the vastness that seemed to be bursting within my brain. I conceived the idea of using this Universal Mind like a lending library. Maybe I could let it all go there and then retrieve it in smaller bits so that my mind could handle it piece by piece.

Once I formulated this idea, the visions began to release themselves from within my head, and over the years, I have indeed been able to retrieve thoughts from The Universal Mind. It has become the foundation of my own philosophy and I have been learning from those visions ever since.

The depth contained within my kitchen in those few moments, and the visions that sent me running from the house, stretched beyond time and space. Nothing that I have seen in my life has given me more understanding. No Guru, Church, nor written word has ever been able to tell me more truth. Truth experienced is so different from truth told or read. Words are so limiting and I had paid for this truth with my blood.

It was Friday, work was finished and people were going home for the weekend. "Thank God it's Friday at last," I heard a secretary say. I didn't think too much about it until the following Monday when I found myself on the same elevator with the same secretary. "Oh God," she said. "Another Monday and another week of work." This person loathed a full third of the life she was living. Something snapped inside of me and I determined that I was not going to allow myself to end up in a similar situation.

Although I didn't realize it, I was changing. I was seeing myself through different eyes. I knew that I was unhappy with my situation but how could I change my life? How could I change myself? I felt stuck in my job, in my home, in my life and with responsibilities. There had to be a way I could find freedom.

Four A.M. in my office at Gibraltar Savings and Loan. Since I could choose my own hours I worked in the quiet hours of the early morning. One morning the idea came to me to give my house and my belongings away; if I gave the house away I would be free both of the house and the responsibilities that accompanied it. This would also allow me to quit my job and find freedom. I decided to give my house to a group of my old friends. It was my hope that with my gift they would learn to share with one another and learn to love one another like my hippie friends loved each other. So I did quit my job. Several things happened that delayed the transfer of the house and I was to stay in my home for a few more months.

Although I was determined to follow through with my plan, there was a small nagging fear of what was to going to happen to me. In the months leading up to my actual departure, I would find myself sleeping or napping with my thumb grasped between my fingers as a child might to soothe and feel protected. When I noticed this, I would gently remove my thumb from within my fingers. It made things seem more difficult to face, yet it made it more permanent somehow.

I had my truck and money was not a problem, so I was able to help when people needed to move large things. Some of my new friends were moving around from one place to another at that time and I helped many of them move. I also began cooking for anyone who happened to drop by at dinner time.

Someone once asked how I could afford to feed so many people since I didn't have an income anymore. I took her to a spare room off of the kitchen, the breakfast room. There was a player piano in it which we used to play, and sing songs. It was fun. Now, piled in the center of the room were stacks upon stacks of boxes of food. There was food piled everywhere in the room. "I don't dare stop feeding people," I told her. "Food keeps coming in and if I don't use it, it will end up filling the room." It seemed that whenever I would move someone they would generally give me the food that they did not take with them.

One day I was helping a friend move. John was with me and we were joined by Karen, one of the hippies. All day we moved truckloads of stuff from one house to the other.

The place our friend was moving into was high up on a hill and there was a hairpin turn about halfway up. All day long I had tried to make it past this turn without having to jog my way through, but I wasn't able to do it. My truck simply could not turn sharply enough to make the switchback, so I always had to back up and maneuver my way passed the turn.

The day was ending and it was to be our last trip up the mountain. Coming to the turn, I thought, *"It's my turn."* All day long I had given in to the mountain. Now it was just "my turn," nothing more, nothing less. I turned the wheel as far as I could and drove on. Moving forward it became obvious that I was going to run into the mountain, but I continued to drive anyway. *"It's my turn,"* I thought again.

There was no challenge in my action, no waving of hands nor bellowing out loud, just one part of the universe with another. I simply drove around the turn without stopping or slowing down.

Then the mountain "just was" about three feet or so farther back and I continued driving through as if there had been plenty of space to begin with. "Nice job of moving the mountain, Michael," John said. Karen gulped, "Did you see that?" I don't think I said much other than perhaps, "Yup." Miracles happen all the time, but they seldom appear to those who are not prepared to witness them.

Finally the big day arrived. I was to leave the house for the last time. I had loaded my truck with extravagant gifts: crystal, china, paintings, bits of furniture and nicknacks; gifts that through the process of giving them away would set me free. I had wanted to leave by noon; no special reason, I was just used to a schedule. I was rushing through the house working myself into a panic. Marshall was helping, but also watching me. "Michael," he said, "no one knows you are coming, you are not expected. You don't have to leave at any certain time. Why don't you take a long, hot bath?" I realized that he was right. No one did expect me and there really wasn't any reason to rush. So I did take a long, hot bath before I left. The bath did wonders for me and I was able to leave with plenty of daylight left. Later, driving across the desert north of Los Angeles, I took my watch off and threw it out onto the desert floor. I have never worn a watch since. Indeed, I have gained a fairly accurate feeling for time and seldom have need of a clock.

I was giving away all I had. I drove all around the West, visiting friends and family and leaving gifts like the legendary Santa Clause. Most of the things I gave away I have never missed, including the house. A few things, however, like some of the furniture that I had made, I did miss for a time. I always thought I would be able to make them again. But a good lesson that I learned is that one seldom travels the same pathway twice. I was never to recreate any of the furniture that I had given away.

I really didn't know what I was going to do now. I had given my house away with no place to go and entered into a new life with no place to hide. But some friends, who I will call Joseph and Joan, took me in. I took care of the house and cooked for the family in lieu of rent.

As a computer programmer, I had made a very good salary. I always had extra money taken out for paying taxes at the end of the year. It wasn't long until I received a $1500 refund check from my taxes; that was a considerable amount of money in 1971. I decided to get it changed into $50 bills, and give them out at street corners.

"No, you're not," Joseph said, "Come with me." He took me to a travel agent that he had met at work and had me buy a round-trip ticket to London— $175 on People's Airline. You had to bring your own bagged meal, but it was cheap. I also bought a two week Brit pass for unlimited travel around Great Britain and a three month Eurail pass which gave me unlimited first class travel on trains and ships all over free Europe.

At the time I didn't realize that it was only after I had given everything away and was penny-less that I was able to go to Europe.

Chapter 4

Europe and God's Socks

Now I had totally changed my life; I had given everything away and quit my job. There was no turning back, not that I wanted to, I was excited about going to Europe.

Mike, the programmer might have gone to Europe for two weeks on vacation, (maybe, but probably not). But Michael the free spirit with no possessions and only an income tax refund in his hands, was off to Europe for four months!

What I didn't know was that when I came back to the States, I was not to see my friends the hippies again.

My hippie friends were very supportive of my trip to Europe and were wishing me well. The night before I was to leave they asked to borrow a pair of my Levis that they said they would bring to the airport.

Mary, James and John met me at the airport. They gave me some gifts. They also brought my Levis, with "Love Me" embroidered on the back. There was a medal pinned to one front pocket. They also gave me a beautiful chain with a dove of peace on a six-pointed star in silver, hanging from the chain. The six-pointed star remained for me, a symbol of hard fought truth. I still have that emblem from my friends the hippies.

I landed in London where I was to meet the first of very few obstacles to face me on this trip. There was "no room in the inn." There was some kind of convention in London and all rooms seemed to be booked up.

I was not then, nor am I now, a very good planner when I make trips. Things like where I'll stay or when I'll arrive seem to be too stringent for me to think about beforehand.

I walked around London as much as I could, looking for a place to stay. I finally decided to go to Victoria station, catch an overnight train to Liverpool, and take the overnight ship to Dublin, Ireland.

Michael Jonas, my best friend, had an aunt who lived in Dublin. She had spent several weeks in California earlier that year. When she had over-stayed her welcome at her sister's house, I let her stay with me. "If you're ever in Ireland," she said, "please come and stay with me." I took her at her word.

When I got to Victoria station, my feet were hurting a bit. I had bought a brand new pair of boots before I left Los Angeles and had not broken them in yet, so I was just breaking them in now. I arrived at the station to find that the train to Liverpool would not leave until the next morning.

There was nothing for me to do but to stretch out on a bench in the station and get some rest. After a 14 hour flight and several hours walking around London looking for a place to stay, I was tired.

Sleep barely closed my eyes when I felt a not too gentle tap on my foot. The first word I learned in "Great Britain English" was "Bobbie," the British word for policeman. There was one standing over me. "You can't sleep here," he said. "Move on."

So it was that the first night of my stay in Europe, England actually, I walked the streets of London in new boots; walking and waiting until time for the train to leave in the morning. I did see the Tower of London, Buckingham palace and the changing of the Guard. I even heard an early morning boys choir practicing in a church before I boarded the train at last. Aboard the train I was finally able to sleep for an hour or so.

I had called my friend's aunt from London the previous evening and told her that I was on my way, so I was expected. When I got to Dublin and her house, however, I found it deserted. There was no one home. I sat on the front porch for an hour or so, waiting. Still she didn't arrive. I noticed that the grass was about 8 or 9 inches long so I went into the garage, which I found unlocked. I found her lawnmower and with a great deal of effort I cut her overgrown grass. After that I sat again on the front porch.

A neighbor across the street had been watching me. After I cut the grass and was waiting again, she called across the road and introduced herself. She asked me who I was and what I was doing there. I explained my situation. "I'll bet she's gone to O'Brian's Bridge to stay with her family," she said. "She's probably afraid that people will talk if a man stays in her house with her." (She did not have a very good opinion of my friend's aunt.)

Later, she asked me to come across the street to her house where she had fixed me a wonderful dinner. (It hadn't escaped me that it had been two days since I had eaten a decent meal.) That night I slept in Mike's aunt's garage. After the previous night in London and trying to sleep on the train, then again on the overnight boat, the garage felt like a wonderful and welcoming place to stay. I passed out and slept about 18 hours.

When I awoke, I again sat on the front steps, wondering

what to do next. The lady across the street again invited me over, this time for breakfast. My first taste of Irish breakfast was sausage, bacon, ham and eggs. How wonderful it tasted! She was a very nice lady and not at all happy with what she felt was cowardice on the part of her neighbor across the street.

I told her that I felt it was best if I just left and went back to England; I did not want to make my friend's aunt uncomfortable. I had not had a shower since I had left the U.S.A. three days earlier, so I did ask if I could take a bath. "But it's not Thursday," she said. She finally did let me take a wonderful hot bath. The tub was short but deep and I luxuriated in the warm water that surrounded and relaxed me.

Then, giving her a set of love beads that I had made for her, I left Ireland.

Arriving in England again, I began to use my 14 day "Brit pass," a prepaid ticket on all of England's trains and buses. I travelled mostly in the northern part of England, finding places to stay in the youth hostels that abounded in the countryside. I would just go to places and walk about the streets.

Once, some guys were pushing a stalled car to get it started. I ran out and helped them push. Later I heard two ladies walking in front of me chatting with themselves. "I've cleaned me heart out today," one said. Nodding back, her friend replied, "Ai, but you'll get no medals for it." So I reached down and took the medal off of my "Love Me" Levis. I went to her and said, "I think you deserve a medal." I pinned it upon her, gave her a hug, and walked back along the street with a big smile in my heart.

Walking had become a bit of a challenge for me. Because of breaking in my new boots while tramping around the streets of London, I had bloody blisters on my feet. But I did keep walking around and seeing things. It took about a month for the blisters to heal and toughen enough for me to enjoy walking again, but in spite of my feet I did keep getting out and seeing the usual sights of the north-east english cities and countryside.

After my tour in England, I took the boat from Dover to Calais in France. There I began a three month tour of Europe by rail. In those days, a first-class three month ticket only cost about $175. A lot of hippies and other "free" types were doing the same thing then, so no matter where I went, I usually ran into some people from the States.

It didn't take me long to figure out that in the first-class cabins, the seats could be pulled out to meet the opposite seat in the middle, making a very comfortable bed. So when night came, if I had no place to stay, I would go to the train station, find an overnight train to anywhere, (mostly in a different country), and I would talk all of my cabin mates into pulling our seats together so we could sleep comfortably. Most of the people I met (other than other traveling hippies) were a bit standoffish with others in the cabin. But with my encouragement, the resistance usually melted away and a communal bed was made for the night. We all wanted to sleep anyway, so feet in each others faces, we slept the night away to wake up in another country.

The Eurail pass allowed me to go to 16 different countries and principalities in Western Europe. I went to all the countries except one. For some reason I could never get a good connection to visit Luxembourg. I took pride in visiting the smaller principalities of Andorra and Monaco.

I even took a two-day train trip just to get to the Principality of Liechtenstein. Liechtenstein is smaller than Washington, D.C; so small that when the train going cross country leaves a station, it has to stop to give the conductor time to collect tickets before entering the next town. I figured that I traveled around 39,000 miles in the three months I had my pass: (I did use the trains as beds very often), from the South in Torremolinos, Spain to north of the Arctic circle in Narvic, Norway, and from the East in Calais, France, to the West in Vienna, Austria.

On the train to Torremolinos I met an older English professor traveling with his granddaughter. We chatted about my travels and when we arrived at the station I took my leave of them.

Walking along I noticed the sound of footsteps following me. I turned around to see the professor and his granddaughter behind me.

"Are you following me"? I inquired.

"You will find a place to stay tonight, won't you?" the Professor answered.

"I guess I will, I always seem to," I replied.

"That's why we are following you," he returned. I did Indeed find us a place to spend the night. In appreciation, the Professor asked me to join him and his granddaughter for dinner.

He told me that the meal was to be at his expense and that he wanted to do the ordering. When the meal came it looked somewhat like deep fried onion rings. "I'm not going to tell you what they are," he told me. Taking a huge bite, his granddaughter told me, "These are octopus tentacles."

I had made a vow to myself that I would eat whatever was presented to me on this trip, something that I continue to do as I travel around the world. If I don't like something, I don't have to eat it, but for the most part I've enjoyed almost everything I've tried. Octopus and squid have become some of my favorite foods.

After a few days I was ready to leave southern Spain. A train was scheduled to leave about 6 a.m. the next morning and I decided to get up early and be on my way. There was a clock on the wall in my room, but I didn't have an alarm clock and they did not provide wake up calls so I wasn't sure that I would make it but I'd try.

In the darkness just before dawn I awakened from a dream; I was waving from the window of a fast moving train. I turned on the light and looked at the clock—there was just enough time to get ready and make it to the station. After throwing my watch out into the desert a few months earlier, I was pleased at the realization that I had developed a pretty good sense of internal time.

The trip back up through Spain was long and hot. The first class cabin was almost full. In the cabin was a woman with her daughter, a friendly old man with a large bag, a well dressed woman, and me.

After the train pulled out from the shade of the station and the heat began to beat down on us the well dressed woman pulled a bottle of water from her bag and drank surreptitiously, then eased the bottle back into her bag. A while later the mother reached into a sack, pulled out two pieces of chicken, and gave one to her daughter. They ate, shielding their food almost as if in secret, and yet we were in an open cabin.

The old man, kind of battered looking and travel worn, took a bottle of wine from his bag. He opened it, took a drink then with a smile, passed it around the cabin for us all to share. I remembered the same ritual used when I was sharing water with my friends, the hippies.

I then took out my bag of beads and thread. "Love beads" were the thing of the day. I made many of them during my trip around Europe; they were my "thank you" gifts. I showed the beads to the old man sharing wine, and with gestures, (since I didn't speak Spanish,) I let him know that I was going to make him a necklace and that he was to choose the colors that he liked. He was embarrassed but he did choose some colors.

The Mother took another piece of chicken and sneaked it to her daughter and to herself, and the well dressed woman drank her water, again secretly. The old man took another drink of wine and passed it around the cabin.

When I finished the Love beads for the old man, I gave them to him and gestured to the lady sitting next to him (the one with the water). Showing her the different colored beads in my bag I let her know that I was going to make one for her as well. She chose her colors. As I began to string her beads I made it known that I would make everyone in the cabin a set of love beads before we arrived in Barcelona in the morning.

Then the Mother took another piece of chicken from her bag, went to hand it to her daughter, but then she paused and handed it to me. She reached again into her bag and brought out a piece for her daughter, but as she reached over she hesitated, then shrugged and offered it to the old man instead.

In the end, she offered each of us a piece of the welcomed meat. The nicely dressed lady had several bottles of water and she offered each of us drinks from her bottles. The old man kept us supplied with wine. Soon everyone brought out bits and pieces of food to share and we all had a wonderful and fulfilling meal with wine and water, and in the morning as we entered the Barcelona station, I tied the knot on the very last set of love beads.

I decided that since Torremolinos was the southernmost part of Europe that I would be visiting, I would go from there to the northernmost part that was accessible by train; which according to my railway map, was above the Arctic Circle at Narvik, Norway. I was excited to think that I would be able to see the Northern lights.

Changing trains somewhere in Germany, I met a girl named Joan. She was British from South Africa. She was wearing a long winter coat and was surrounded by about ten suitcases of varying sizes. Both of us were headed to Narvik, and in the way of foreign travelers, we decided to team up. I pointed out that I carried a rather heavy back pack containing all of my belongings and that I would not be carrying any of her luggage.

I was heading to Amsterdam to get some money, so I suggested that she go there with me and check most of her bags at the Central Station. This, she decided, was a good idea. After checking most of her luggage we were off to Narvik. Our journey took us up through northern Germany and into Denmark, where we spent some time sight seeing. We saw several sights including the statue of the "Little Mermaid." Over her head we saw a very be-flagged boat coming into the harbor, and were treated by seeing King Frederick IX of Denmark returning to his capital. From Copenhagen we crossed over into Sweden.

In Stockholm we met a young Swedish guy named Torbijorn (Tor-be-own). Torbijorn was on his way to Narvik as well, so the three of us teamed up. Like so many people in Europe, Torbijorn spoke excellent English which was a treat for both Joan and myself. Torbijorn told us that there was a railroad that went even farther north than Narvik into a small town called Fläm which is situated at the very end of the Sognefjord, one of the longest and deepest of the fjords in Norway. Of course we changed our destination.

Our route took us up the entire length of Eastern Sweden. Mostly what I remember of that passage was the tremendous amount of pine trees. After crossing over the Arctic Circle we passed into Norway at Narvik. From here we boarded the Fläm railway which would take us on what is considered one of the most beautiful train trips in the world, and among the steepest. The trip was indeed wonderful. We went past beautiful huge and varied waterfalls and landscapes so green and lush that they could only happen in the moist northern countries.

Our trip ended in Flam. Joan wanted to stay in a hotel but Torbijorn and I wanted to sleep in a tent. We made our camp at the very end of the Sognefjord. There was a wonderful view of blue water so clear we could see the bottom of the fjord as it reached far away from us. On either side rose bright green gentle hills. What a great place to camp!

We all met for dinner then took a ski lift up to the top of a mountain to see the midnight sun. During the time it took to sip a cup of coffee, the sun set in front of us, only to rise again a few minutes later from the same spot. Rather spectacular in itself but when I asked about the Aurora Borealis, I was disappointed to find that during the late summer, what we got was what we had just seen: the midnight sun. The Aurora happened only in the winter.

Over the course of the evening, Torbijorn told me that his plan was to take a rubber boat that he had carried with him) down the entire length of the Sognefjord to Oslo. I immediately wanted to go with him and he liked the idea as well, so in the morning I told Joan that I would not be joining her on her trip back to Amsterdam. She was incensed and demanded that I take her back as she had no idea how to find her luggage. Even after telling her that anyone in Amsterdam Central could show her, she still demanded, and she won.

As I look back on that time, I realize that I turned away from what might have been my greatest adventure because not only did Joan insist, she expected. me take her back as well. She had created a place for me in her immediate life, and pictured me in it. In her arrogance, Joan merely ignored my own one-of-a-kind adventure simply because she felt she might be inconvenienced. This is much like how the British treated the Africans during their occupation of South Africa. They just expected them to act in a certain way, and they did. While Joan was firm in her expectation, I was still "just traveling around without plans," therefore, vulnerable to outside suggestion. Then again, there was the fact that I was also very polite.

Desire and expectation; combined with action are very powerful tools. They are the same tools that I used to make the mountain move not so many months before, and the tools that Joan was now using on me. I have also used those tools with success many times as the years have gone by.

I arrived in Vienna, Austria, late one night only to find that there were no trains scheduled to leave or arrive until morning. A girl was standing in the middle of the station. I was trying to read the train schedules but was confused. I went up to the girl and asked, "Is Agfart going out or is Agfunt going out?" She did not know either. She was also an American so we decided to pool our chances.

As we left the station a cab driver found us. "Do you want a place to spend the night?" He asked. "Yup." So it was, that we found ourselves at the cab driver's house. His mother had a wonderful room in the attic with a big high bed, thick with blankets on top of a mattress that was even thicker. After showing us around, the young man who was the cab driver pushed a few times on the bed to show us that it squeaked. Smiling, he then went to bed, leaving us to sleep, without squeaking the bed.

In the morning, his mother fixed us a wonderful breakfast and he showed us all around Vienna. We saw the Vienna woods, twin palaces and other places that we just saw, but did not have time to really get to know.

Such was my first trip to Europe: going to and through places and countries, mostly in search of a place to sleep or a name on a map. In places where there were Youth Hostels, I took the opportunity to look around, peek into corners and walk down back streets. I really didn't know a lot about European countries before I left the States and although I knew a bit more after leaving those countries, there was so very much more I could have learned and experienced.

Amsterdam, Holland was my base in Europe. I had money sent there a bit at a time. That way if I lost my wallet I wouldn't lose all of my money. So when I ran out of money I would catch a train to Amsterdam and get more money at the American Express office. I came to know Amsterdam and Rotterdam very well during my stay in Europe.

I was getting some money in Amsterdam when I saw in the papers that in Sicily, Mount Etna was erupting. Since I had never seen a volcano erupting, I got on a train and went across Europe and down through Italy to take a boat to Sicily. I set up my tent on a beach in Taormina within sight of Mount Etna, which was smoking, disappointingly, instead of spewing lava.

I met some young locals on the beach however, who lived in the nearby town. My tent was situated near a couple from Rotterdam. Lous and Lewis were very friendly and Lewis invited me to stay with him when I got back to Holland. He and Lous were just dating then but were planning to get married when they could get a license to get a larger apartment together. I took him up on his invitation and stayed with him several times after that.

Venturing into Taormina, I met a young man who took a liking to me. People from the United States seldom made their way to Sicily so I was a bit of a novelty. Angelo had a dinner party to welcome me and I was able to meet several of his friends who were also interested in welcoming a traveling hippy from the States. Angelo spent the day diving for our dinner. He caught some squid, octopus and a large bag of mussels. I wanted to help with dinner, so Angelo let me stir the sauce while he went about his other chores.

At one point he told me to open my mouth; he then opened a mussel and scraped it on my lower teeth. This was pretty good, so when I stopped stirring I reached my hand in the bag and brought out a mussel. I pried it open but it shut again. I pried it open again only to find that again it closed. It was alive! This was one thing I could not, and still will not do, to eat a creature while it is alive. So I put it back into the bag and enjoyed the rest of the dinner.

One of my favorite memories of Taormina was walking down the sleepy main street and hearing. "Ciao Michaeli" shouted from an upstairs window. "Ciao Franco," I yelled back. What a homey and welcoming experience; and I was almost 7,000 miles from home.

Traveling back up through Italy, I had wanted to stop in Florence and was following my map which was in English. The station sign was not; "*Firenze*" said the sign. *Must be the next stop*, I thought. When the train was about to leave the station, someone pointed out that Firenze was the Italian name for Florence and I jumped from the train just as it began to move.

Walking down the ancient streets in Florence I saw small

children running in and out of renaissance houses that had the Medici crest carved above the door. Such places, anywhere else in the world would, become a museum. In Firenze they were just, - home.

Florence was one of the places where I was able to stay in a Youth Hostel, so I was able to explore to my heart's content. Of course I also saw the more famous sights and museums of Firenze, but I liked walking on small cobbled streets or down alleyways. Strange, whenever I visit a foreign country now, I still like to leave the busy streets and explore the small streets or roads and especially alleyways.

Walking down an alley in Florence one day, I saw an ancient Roman statue standing amid a garden in back of a home. The statue was leaning a bit as it had not been properly placed. So many of the people of Florence live side by side with the remnants of the Renaissance. Here these things would be treasures. There?

I had brought things to give: small presents like my love beads or xeroxed copies of my little book, *Me, my brother and I.* Although I gave my small gifts without thought of receiving, I found many times that my unspoken needs were fulfilled.

Several times I was hungry and people just gave me food. Twice when I was out of cigarettes, people simply bought me a pack without asking or being asked for them. I'm glad to say that I gave up that habit years ago. But how these people knew that I wanted a cigarette, I'll never know, or that I was hungry for that matter.

One time I was sharing a cabin with a very well-dressed woman. I was a hippie and looked the part with my back pack and worn clothing. She was so clean and tidy with her hair neatly tied back in a bun. For her, riding in a first-class cabin set her apart from the norm. For me, it was just the way it happened. I sat for quite awhile across from her, almost afraid of offending her with any sound or movement. Finally I got bored and reached into my pack, pulled out my beads, and began to make a set of love beads. "You are a very remarkable young man," the lady said to me. She spoke perfect English, although I think she was German.

As we talked I felt that she might like to read my little booklet, so I gave her a copy. After a time she looked up from the book with tears in her eyes and said, "I see so much of myself in your book."

Then she left the compartment and came back with some apples which she gave me. I had been hungry but hadn't said anything about it. She also gave me a package of cigarettes, although she didn't know that I smoked and had been longing for one. She didn't smoke herself.

Another time in another train in Italy, I had given a set of love beads to a rather ragged old man. He got tears in his eyes, left the compartment, and came back with a package of cigarettes for me. He couldn't speak English and I couldn't speak Italian but somehow he knew. He ripped off the entire top of the package to show me that these cigarettes had filters.

Often, when I went to Amsterdam to get money, I would also stop to see or stay with Lewis whom I had met in Sicily. He, Lous and I became friends and had good times when we were together. Lewis had a motorcycle, as did the majority of people in Rotterdam, and all over Europe for that matter. When we went out I always rode on the back. One day Lewis called over his shoulder, "The rain always stops when you are riding with me, did you know that?" As a matter of fact, I did not know that. I did know that it was raining a lot whenever I was in Rotterdam, but somehow it had escaped me that when we were riding in the streets there was never rain.

As happened several times during my trip, I was at a loss as to where to go next. Sometimes too many choices are more of a problem than a solution. Lewis suggested that I visit his sister in Vienna. My previous trip had been rather a whirl-wind of sights from the inside of a taxi. Visiting his sister would allow me to spend a few days and finally see the city. Lewis called his sister and it was arranged.

Lewis' sister Anke, was a delight. We enjoyed our time together and I, "flush" with a little money from home, took her to dinner. Other times she enjoyed showing off her cooking for me. One day we spent the afternoon chatting and drinking beer. That evening we went out for a walk and found a sign that sported some pine branches. It said, *Ausg'steckt"* I think. Anke said that it meant the new wine was ready and being served. We went into the wine tavern and had a glorious evening. The wine was great and the company was wonderful.

I was planning to leave in the morning but when the dawn came, I was as sick as I have ever been in my life (that I can remember). As my friend Yvette would say, "Beer before wine, nein." When I recovered, (which seemed like forever) I took the next train out, which took me into Germany.

Sitting on a hill alongside the railroad tracks and eating bread, salami and cheese, I could hear loudspeakers calling orders (I suspect) to the workers. The rail yard was busy with trains shuttling cars from one place to another. The yard was a beehive of activity. Closing my eyes and listening to the sounds, I went back to the time when Germany was at war. The vision in my mind was disturbing so I got on a train and left.

I was in Paris, about to take a train back to Amsterdam for what would be the last trip before my three month Eurail pass expired. You could see the panic in some backpackers faces when they realized that the Eurail pass that they had come to depend upon was about to expire. I wasn't in a panic but I did have to make some plans. My return flight was not for another month so I had a month to spend in Amsterdam. I did not know where I would stay, a youth hostel perhaps.

As I was walking past the second-class cars, someone called

out to me. A good looking guy was beckoning to me from the train window, welcoming me to Europe. We talked a minute through his window. I had wished for someone who could speak English. He did. I told him that I would pay the difference for him to ride in First class with me. He was going to Amsterdam, too. His name was Hans and he was Dutch. So many Dutch speak perfect English.

We had a great visit during the trip from Paris to Amsterdam, and I was very excited to be able to chat with someone in English, at last. When we arrived in Amsterdam, Hans invited me to stay in his house with his wife, Mira and his daughter, Ellis. Mira was crippled with arthritis and needed help to get around so I ended up helpeing Hans and his family for the month remaining before my flight back home.

During the month I was in Amsterdam I lived much like the Dutch: I went to the market and bought the food for the day, cooked our meals, did the cleaning and washing and even took little Ellis to school in the mornings.

It was, and still is, legal to smoke pot and hash in the Netherlands. Many of the evenings Hans would take me to the hash houses: The Milky Way (although it wasn't spelled that way) and the Paradiso were our favorites. The hash houses we visited had many rooms, each with a different theme to help people enjoy their "trip." Some rooms were playing comical slide shows.

I remember one showed many of the various bridges in Amsterdam opening and closing in sequence. A bridge would be pictured closed in the down position, followed by a picture of the same bridge opened with a boat coming underneath. Then the pictures would be repeated opening then closing, quickly repeating the action. If you were stoned it was hilarious.

On a similar theme, there was a reclining female nude with a hand modestly covering her groin, followed by a similar one where the hand would be placed on her hip. Then the pictures would be quickly repeated so the action was like watching a peep show. Each room had different ways of getting stoned visitors into peals of laughter.

Near the end of my stay in Amsterdam, Hans pulled up his prize pot plant that was growing in his garden. It was only about 1 foot or so tall and sort of scrawny. Hans, Mira and Helmuth, a German hippie that we knew, were going to have dinner and smoke this small plant. It was to give its all for us.

I had always suspected that it is not as much the power of the plant itself but the combined energy of the people smoking it that make a "good trip" happen. That evening in Amsterdam, the little plant sent us all on a very special journey.

After a few hours, Hans and Mira went to bed. Helmuth asked me to join him in the Vondel park where he had his sleeping bag. I wanted to go with him because I liked Helmuth. However I just felt too stoned to go out, and besides, I did not want Hans and Mira to wake up and find me gone. So Helmuth departed and I was left alone with nothing to do.

It occurred to me that this would be a very good time to darn the holes in my socks. I had bought very good socks when I had left the States, almost four months earlier. The new boots that had worn bloody blisters on my feet had also worn holes in several of my socks as well. This was the perfect time to do some mending.

Although I had never done this before, I began darning my socks. My mind went away. I remembered the acid trip I had taken when I had realized that man and God were one. I smiled at the fear that I had experienced with that realization.

Suddenly, it occurred to me that if this were true, I was darning God's socks! I was terrified and began to shake. *How could I possibly darn God's socks?* I was not up to the task. I could not possibly do such a thing. Then I remembered a time when I was on a "trip" where I had expanded outward to become the infinite universe. I had been afraid that I would explode up and out into nothingness. Then I had "turned around" and focused instead on the inside; becoming the tiny spot was also me—the God/god.

So I forced myself to become the God part, darning the socks of Michael the Hippie. As I darned the socks, I began to think of the bloody feet that had worn these socks as they walked alone in the streets of London. (The boots that had given me such pain before were broken in now.)

As I darned the socks I cried for that poor guy and for his pain. The tears I shed, fell onto the socks as I darned. There was a fuzziness that happened as the tears blended with the threads, and I had trouble seeing what I was doing. Finally I finished and went to bed. Though I searched later, very hard, I was never able to find the place where the socks were darned.

My home off and on for three months looked like this.

Edinburgh, Scotland

No matter where I travelle in Europe
my wardrobe seldom changed.

Myrdal, Norway

When I returned to the United States I had changed. I was not the same person and I had not wanted to be.

I had traveled to places where I could not speak the language, but the language of love and giving had seen me through. I had gone without a guide, without a plan and without real security. Although I Had felt exceptionally vulnerable when my three month Eurail pass expired. I had lived each day unto itself knowing that somehow I would eat, enjoy and find a place to sleep, and I did. I had grown in ways I never would have thought possible. I still give thanks for that time as I travel around the world where I know little or none of the language.

Love Me levies

Chapter 5

Michael the Carpenter

Without very much planning on my part, life seemed to be working out for me. The leap of faith that I had taken when I gave everything away, called "stepping out," by the hippies, had rewarded me with a four month trip to Europe.

When I got back from my trip, I again joined Joseph, Joan and their family.

I had given everything away, except my tools. I loved to work with wood and with tools, plus I was handy around the house. I kept the tools so I could create a new life for myself when I "stepped back in."

I arrived back in California with gifts for Joseph, Joan and their family. Many times on my trip I had gone without so I could buy presents for them. They welcomed me back into their home and I was treated like a member of the family. I have always liked keeping busy, so I did the cooking and cleaning to pay for my keep. I also made minor repairs about the house as I found work that needed to be done.

I had a lot of tools and was able to do plumbing, electrical work and mechanical repairs as well as my favorite projects, which involved working with wood. Few things made me as happy as when I was building something that I had designed. As Christmas approached I made small gifts out of wood for my friends. I even created an old fashioned outhouse as a wrapping for a lathe that I gave to Joseph. It was much more interesting than wrapping paper and was a center-piece of conversation when guests came visiting.

Christmas came and went. Now spring was coming and I wasn't too sure what to do next. I knew that I had to do something to make myself a new life. Joseph, Joan and the family made me feel welcome, but sleeping on the couch and not making any money of my own was beginning to feel uncomfortable and I wanted to create a life for myself again. Perhaps a little bit of reality was seeping back into the vision of my life.

Then I met Ed. Ed had a desire to make an arts and crafts store in the mountains; a place where local people could bring their art to sell on consignment. He had rented a log cabin in Mountain Center, a town of 80 people located in the mountains above Palm Springs, California. Ed worked as a cook down the hill in Hemet, at a "fat farm" or spa, where rich women went to lose weight.

His desire was to quit his job, stay in the mountains and run his store. He just wasn't sure how to go about making his dream come true. What he needed was someone to turn his cabin into an arts and crafts store, a person who could both design and build it for him. When we met each other it took no time at all before we found that I was exactly what he needed and his situation was perfect for me to begin my new life.

I had always loved being in the mountains. Now, not only was I going to be able to live in them, I was going to be able to make my living by designing and building with wood at the same time. I couldn't have been happier. This seemed too good to be true.

Excited about my new life, I began to pack my few remaining belongings. But when I started to take my radial arm saw, Joseph started to cry. During the time I was in Europe, he had built a work table around it and made up his mind that my saw was to be his.

When I gave my belongings away I had given Joseph and Joan a lot of things that I would never be able to replace. I had wanted to get rid of everything that tied me to my "old life." None of my tools however, were ever in question; especially my radial arm saw which I used a great deal.

In quitting my job and giving everything away, I had "stepped out," or left the mainstream of life as I had known it. "Stepping back in" meant that I would once again take up the responsibility of earning a living. Working with my hands and my tools were going to be the way I would create my new life, for I knew I did not want to go back into programming.

Joseph and I had discussed my need for the tools before I left for Europe and he knew of my passion for working with wood. How, I wondered, did he expect me to make a living without my saw. No matter how long I talked, Joseph would not listen to reason. He was devastated and acted as if I had betrayed him.

We finally ended up agreeing that I would borrow my saw and give it back as soon as I could afford to replace it. Joseph was making a lot of money at that time as a computer systems analyst. I was making nothing. The saw only cost about $200. He could easily have afforded to buy his own. But he exchanged the saw for my friendship instead.

I moved to Mountain Center above Palm Springs and just

down the road from Idyllwild, a quaint mountain tourist town. Thus, Mike the programmer, then Michael the hippie turned into Michael the carpenter.

The first few months I spent cleaning out and repairing the cabin in preparation for the transformation into an art store. Ed was supplying me with food and shelter in exchange for the work.

Tom knew that I was handy with tools so when "the spa" needed some work, Tom recommended me. I worked for three or four weeks for them, doing odd jobs and repairs. I even built a store for them out of a double garage. Soon I had enough money to buy a used truck. I found just what I wanted in the local paper, but the man who was selling the truck would not let me drive it for some reason. He insisted on driving it himself. I didn't think too much about it at the time; I was and still am, very trusting. I bought the truck with cash and drove it away.

Driving into town I tried to shift gears and found the gear shift was stuck. I had to coast into a parking space. Now I knew why the man had sold it to me so cheaply, also why he wouldn't let me drive. He must have thought there was an expensive transmission problem with the truck. After crawling under the truck, I shook a few things and found a bolt with a very loose nut. It was the connection between the gear shift and the transmission. I tightened the nut and it worked perfectly from then on. Things were simpler in those days.

About six months later, Joseph and Joan came to get my radial arm saw. The feelings from them were so cold, so uncaring. They took the saw and I never saw them again. I found an old radial arm saw in the paper for $50. It was not as good as the saw that Joseph took, but it would suffice. A radial arm saw was for me, my most useful tool. Fortunately I now had a truck and could haul it back to the cabin. I loved having a truck and could never have made my life work without one.

One of my friends was an artist who painted for a huge art distributing company. Roy had lived with us in Silverlake before I gave the house away. After visiting me at the cabin one time he suggested that I visit the art store where he worked. They imported ornate, gilded framing material that was shipped in wooden crates from Czechoslovakia. The art store was paying $50 per shipment to have the crates hauled away. My friend thought I could use the crate wood in my work. I have always had a kind of love affair with lumber and immediately I saw the many uses that I could make from these crates. I told them I would haul the crates away for nothing. They loved the idea, of course, and soon I had all the wood I could use. Once again I was grateful to have a truck. Now I could keep myself supplied with an unlimited quantity of free wood.

While I lived in the mountains, the art store was a few hours away in Venice beach, south of Los Angeles, but the trips I was able to make were certainly worth it. The wood was rough cut but could be sanded easily. It was the knots in the wood, however, that really got my attention. They were incredibly unique and colorful.

The crate wood itself was twenty feet long; too long for me to work with easily, but there were those beautiful knots. So I took each board and cut it into usable lengths. If I liked the knots in the board, I would cut them out and put them into a special box. The remaining lumber would be sorted by length onto shelves.

My first project was to build a room for myself in the basement so I could have some privacy. After that, I began creating display units out of the crate wood, often incorporating macramé into the design. Each unit was an art piece and I was really proud of the work. Mountain Center Arts and Crafts was coming along just fine. I found that I had knack for design and have enjoyed designing then building something with wood ever since.

When I found spare time, I would work on art projects for myself. The beautiful knots became the first project. I squared them off and glued them together onto plywood, then framed them with crate wood and made what I called, "knot paintings." They were both unique and impressive.

Me inside arts and crafts shop with "knot painting" in back.

And making a built in desk at Harlow Haven

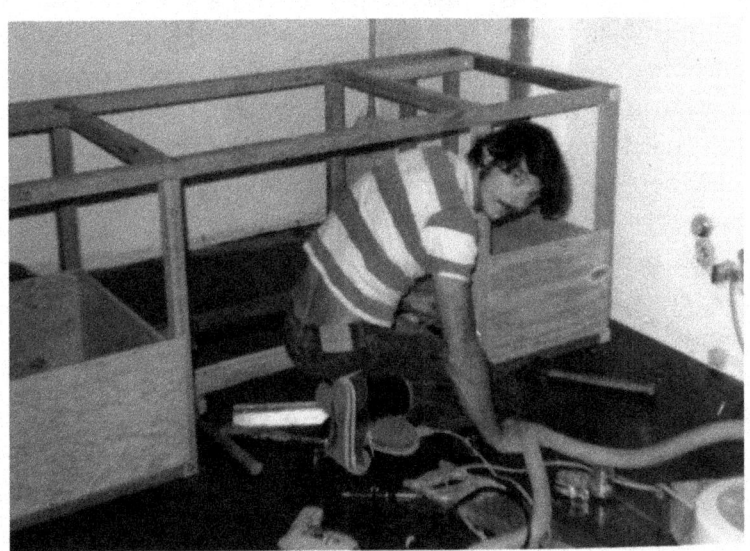

Soon I found that I could burn some knots with a torch, wire brush the burnt part off and faces would appear from different groupings of knots. Of course, like most of my abstract art, it took a little imagination to see them. I called them, "God's little critters."

I used the crate wood for several varying projects including fences, pieces of furniture, room paneling, wine racks for gifts and more. Then I discovered Manzanita burls. These are wonderfully shaped root growths that almost beg to be made into pieces of art. Burnt with a torch, then brushed off, they became pipes, candle holders or art just for the sake of art itself. My wooden art pieces seemed to have a life of their own, with their own personality.

During this time I created a company called, "The Shop – Originals." I was very happy working with wood. It was how I relaxed during the time I was a programmer. Now it served as a fun way for me to make a living.

It didn't take long to find that there was a guru who had an ashram just down the road from our shop. "*A Guru!*" I thought. Many of the hippies that I had known had one or knew of one, and I had hoped to find one for myself. This one taught a variation of what he called Agni Yoga, visualizing fire in different colors. The colors, he taught, could be used for different purposes. Red fire, for instance, could be used to find parking spaces in crowded Idyllwild, just up the hill. Different colors were used for different purposes.

When the Guru found out what I was doing and that I was a carpenter and artisan he asked if I'd teach some of his students. It seems that he had a sort of vocational school going. I agreed to help him out, so at one of his services he announced that I'd be available to teach any who were interested in carpentry. Although I was self taught, he called me a "Master carpenter." That should have been my first clue.

I did teach a few students about carpentry by having them help with whatever project I was involved with at the time; mostly sanding, my least favorite part of woodworking.

I went to a few of the services down the road but soon became discouraged; the fire that one burnt while visualizing colors, along with accomplishing handy things like finding parking places, was supposedly burning impurities away at the same time. This burning left a residue in the stomach which then needed to be burped up to clear away the ash caused by the burning fire. The more you burped the cleaner you became. Everyone was very proud when they burped. Someone would be speaking and from somewhere in the room there would be a large and deep burp. Everyone would look at the person with pride. After not too many burps I decided that this was not the place was not for me. So, Guru-less, I went back to my work which was more fun when I did it alone, anyway.

Soon the Mountain Center Arts and Crafts store opened. People from all over the mountain brought their art pieces for us to sell. I began running the store while making my own art pieces to sell. Mountain Center is just a small town of 80 people, built where the main road forked off to Idyllwild. It was so small that once I got a post card from a friend addressed to Michael Fleming with only the zip code. The post mistress was not happy and told me not to let it happen again!

Soon I became friends with some people up the road in Idyllwild and I would visit them some nights. The group was spiritual and reminded me of the hippies. They smoked pot too. I imagine that most people "up on the mountain" did as well. I remember a time when I was in a café with a man who, for some reason, was about to send a very negative energy outward. I jumped up and "reached out" with my aura in a fan-like fashion, like the tail feathers of a bird, spread out as a barrier to his energy. I was still very much in touch with the "nether places," as my friend John Coffey would say. The man seemed shocked to be stopped like that, and though there was nothing that anyone could see, I had felt the feelings and it reassured me that I did indeed have a spiritual body that was hanging around about me.

The narrow winding road from Idyllwild to Mountain Center

ran along the side of a fairly steep mountain on one side of the road and a large cliff on the other side. Often while driving home I would go into another world. I could see that my world was being created by my own thoughts. Sometimes my truck would head toward the edge of the road as I drove, lost in my thoughts. The first time this happened I realized that I was about to go over the edge of the cliff. Because I was thinking about my thoughts creating my world, I caused the road to extend in front of the truck, using the tools of desire and expectation again. Gaining control of where I was and what I was doing, I continued to drive home without incident. This happened several times again, and each time with confidence, I would picture the road as expanding out in front of me. It must have worked because I never did go over the edge of the cliff.

During the days, I would run the store and make more pieces of art. I came to know the wood and the knots intimately and had sorted all of my wood and knots into various groups for different projects that I had in mind. I'm not sure if I was more impressed with the beautiful knots or the lengths of wood that I was stacking neatly along the walls on different shelves by size.

Once, a friend said he needed a piece of wood to finish a project he was working on. I immediately got him a piece that perfectly matched his needs. He knew me and had watched me work with wood. He said that it took his breath away when I gave him the piece because he knew how much I loved it.

Ed was the chef at the spa in Hemet where I had worked to earn money to buy my truck. He would bring home food that people had left on their plates for our dinner. I didn't mind. I would just make a stew with it. One day he brought a steak home for his dog. To me, he gave scraps from plates. Although I'm an easy going guy, there is something in me that rebels when I am treated badly. For the most part, I say little or nothing at all. I take it inside and do not make a scene. Yet, it does affect me. It was time to go.

The store was finished anyway and I had received some commissions from "Harlow Haven," a newly renovated motel about to open down the mountain in Palm Springs. It had once been owned by Jean Harlow, the actress. I was to build some furniture for a few rooms which had to be ready for their grand opening. I was working at the Motel when I met Jay.

It was the opening night of the motel. Jay was a guest, I was the carpenter. I thought Jay was a good looking guy. We seemed to get on with each other and before I knew it, he had moved up to Crestline with me.

It turns out that Jay was wanted by the police and needed a place to hide. Mountain Center Arts & Crafts was where he chose to get away from it all.

Chapter 6

Jay and the Motorcycle

C hanges were happening again. I could not stay at Mountain Center once the store was finished; Ed wanted to be by himself. Since I had built some furniture for Harlow Haven, they now hired me to do maintenance around the motel. From this, I learned to be a handyman. It would come in handy in years to come.

MF/BB

Jay had just moved to Mountain Center when I decided to take the job down the hill in Palm Springs. He very happily accompanied me and we moved into a room at the Harlow Haven Motel. Both Jay and I were talented workmen and we were welcomed by Jack, the new owner of the motel. I was still able to make arts and crafts in my spare time and I was happy there, but after six months or so Jay got the urge to move on.

Jay was a "mover." He did not like to stay in one place for long, so we moved on, back up into the mountains again; this time to a small town above San Bernardino named Crestline. Life with Jay was always an adventure. He lived by it and for it.

It was winter when we moved and snow was deep upon the ground. I remember trying to move our refrigerator into the cabin we had rented. Jay just tipped it onto its side and we slid it up the snow packed driveway. Jay liked to take chances.

Just outside of the small kitchen, there was a flat cement slab; the perfect place for my shop. Though it was winter, I built a shop for myself there. First, I built a roof to keep the snow away while I worked; then I built the walls. I even found some large windows that had been discarded, so my shop was always filled with light and had a very nice view as well. It seems that I was always able to figure out how to do things as I went about just creating as I built. I was very proud of my new shop.

We made friends with the realtor who found the cabin for us to rent. Soon he was finding jobs for us around the mountain. With the help of my friend Mike, we were even able to buy carpet wholesale. So we added "installing carpet," to our list of "handy" things that we could do. Jay somehow knew how to do it. We did odd jobs around the mountain and I would make the occasional piece or set of furniture. We were making a living and life seemed good.

There was a woman with whom we became friends. We also did some work for her at times. Often she would invite us in after some work or when we met in the village. We would join her at her home when she would play her piano and we would drink sherry together.

One day she asked us to install a new corrugated tin roof on her house. I told her that we didn't know how to do something like that. She said she had faith in us and insisted that we try. So we did. Corrugated metal is formed in a wavelike pattern that creates little hills and valleys in the metal. The nails that were supplied with the corrugated roofing had little rubber caps attached to them, "to keep any rain from getting through," we surmised. It made sense to us that we should hammer the nails in the little valleys where the metal touched the wooden cross beams of the roof. Confident that the little rubber "cups" on the nails would hold out the rain we put the new roof on her house.

- - Then it started to rain.

The rubber caps on the nails, hammered into the "little valleys" did not hold out the rain. I had been right; we did not know how to install the metal roof. The nails should have been driven into the little hills, not the little valleys. She called us in the middle of the night. Her whole house was leaking. We hurried to her house and crawled onto the roof in the rain putting sealant on all the nail holes. It didn't work. There was rain falling on her grand piano. She was not at all happy and was screaming at me. I pointed at her and said, "I told you we didn't know how to do it." She bit the end of my finger. By reflex, I slapped her cheek. The following day she appeared in the village with a neck brace, and I appeared with my finger wrapped with a very large bandage.

It happened that Jay and I were to go and visit my friend Mike, in San Fernando Valley, just outside of Los Angeles. I had met Mike years earlier in Los Angeles at a party. In the course of chatting he let me know that he was moving the following day. I told him that I had a truck and would be happy to help him. The shock at finding someone so willing to help a stranger set us on the path of becoming best friends.

Mike was the friend who helped us to buy carpeting at a discount. We called him "Little Mike," because he was shorter than me. The day that Jay and I were to leave the mountain to visit Little Mike, was snowy and cold. I got into the truck which Jay had running and heating up. Instead of joining me, Jay told me that he had something to do and that he would meet me the next day at Mike's. He reached over and pushed a tape into the cassette player and waved goodbye. I drove off with Neil

Diamond singing "Until It's Time For You To Go," into my ears and I never suspected a thing as I went alone to visit Mike in Los Angeles.

Jay had disconnected the starter on the truck, so that once I got to Los Angeles and turned the truck off I would not be able to start it again. Jay knew that I would not know how to fix it. That night, while I enjoyed being with Mike and his mom, Anne, Jay was writing bad checks all over the various mountain communities. We were known all over the mountain by that time and he had no trouble cashing the checks.

Jay didn't show up at Mike's the following day, so I called him. I kept calling and no one answered. Of course there was no answer. Jay was gone. I called our friend, the realtor, and asked him to go to the cabin to find out what had happened. He called me back and said he had gone to the cabin; Jay was gone. He had left a note. I quite literally fell apart. I couldn't even stand up. Anne began cursing Jay, calling upon him all manner of threats. I remember crawling to her as she cursed him, begging for her not to judge him. She ranted about Jay for hours. It took a week or so for me to pull myself together, but I finally went back up to Crestline.

The first person I met was the woman with the leaking roof. She begged me to fix her roof. The sheets of corrugated metal had to be removed and turned over so that the nails could be replaced onto the top of the arcs instead of the bottoms. I simply could not do this job by myself. Also, I was still stunned and disoriented by Jay's actions. Looking back, I felt that I had been honest with her about her roof. That is about all anyone can do. Then I began receiving letters from all over the mountain, notices of bad checks; checks in the twenties as well as checks in the hundreds.

I had a friend in Crestline who had an art shop. She was a very positive and happy kind of person, and had a shop where she made everything "Smile." She would paint a used high chair with flowers, or decorate salt and pepper shaker lids or even blocks of wood with flowers. I went to her for help.

I knocked on her door and cried myself in. She knew what had happened, of course, but she let me tell her. As we hugged, she told me that she had a rule in her house. That people could speak negative for only five minutes, then they had to talk about positive things.

I was incensed. How could I possibly tell all that had happened in five minutes? She was very sympathetic and waited for me to begin. So I started to tell her all about Jay and the bad checks, the work on the roof that I could not finish and whatever else I could think of. Minutes went by, yet not quite five minutes, (I was watching the clock). There was a minute or so left, but I had run out of things I really had to say. Strange how limited time helps us find the wings to get to the point. I was able to spend the rest of the evening with her, and smiling with her smiles.

Then the snow came. It snowed for several days. It was the worst snow storm in those mountains in many decades. The roof of the hardware store caved in from the weight of the snow.

I had been living in a cabin that was on a hill overlooking the valley. It was located up a flight of 96 stairs from the road; a long climb on a good day. The cabin itself was located within a natural slope between two mountains. As a result, there was strong updraft coming from the valley below and the snow drifted to more than ten feet high! The news said that the storm was going to last the rest of the week. I did not have much food in the house and I was afraid that I would be stranded there until the end of the storm.

I knew I needed to leave the cabin, but the blizzard was raging outside and I was also afraid that I would get lost in the snow; maybe even freeze to death and cause someone problems. I didn't know what to do so I decided to meditate on the problem, praying in my mind that I would come to the correct decision. By the time I finished the meditation I knew that I should leave. I packed a small bag, put on my heaviest coat and left the cabin.

As I opened the door the snow stopped falling. The snow was very deep, almost as deep as the door was tall. I could not burrow underneath it and wondered how I could get out of the cabin and down to the road. I thought of the stair railing that lined both sides of the stairs down to the road level. Digging out, I finally located one of the railings, climbed on top and made my way down to the road like a tightrope walker on a wooden rail; being kept in balance by the snow that buried my feet.

To my surprise, when I reached the road, I found that it had been recently plowed. I was able to walk freely down the hill to the highway. A car came almost immediately and I thumbed a ride. As I closed the car door the snow began to fall again.

With that; I moved down from the mountain and stayed with Mike and his mom, Anne. Steadily, I was getting over the past events. Then one day Jay came back. He was back in my life just like that. Fool that I was, I accepted him back. I didn't even judge him. I was just glad that he was back. There was neither honesty nor caring in Jay. He pushed his way through life without concern for anyone else. He freely admitted that he was wanted by the police and the FBI as well.

Whenever Jay came into my life, he seemed to take me over and my own life path was left behind. He told me that the FBI was searching for him and his trail would soon lead to Little Mike's. We had to leave in order for him to avoid arrest. "We," oh yes, I would indeed join him, there was no question about that. I like to say that it was love that made me follow Jay, but now I wonder of the choice as I balance the word love with the word co-dependence.

Of course we needed money in order to move. Jay had the perfect answer: checks! He wrote them by the dozen. He even got me to write a few.

Soon we were in Texas. He convinced me that since both of us had written bad checks in another state, that we were wanted by the FBI. His solution was to get a new identity.

Identities were easy to get in those days because birth and death records were not kept at the same place and few were computerized then. All you needed for a birth certificate was the birth date and place, plus the mother's maiden name. Armed with a birth certificate you could get a social security number. We told the people at the social security office that we had been Catholic brothers and that's why we had never applied before. With a birth certificate and a social security number, it is easy to get a drivers license. After a few weeks, Jay and I were officially change to other people. People without a past.

While I was trying to settle down and build a new life for us, Jay was planning to move on; and forced us to do so by writing checks. Before I knew it, we had gone from one coast of the USA to the other and back again. Many times we would find work with the Manpower organization doing some of the most vile and disgusting work I could imagine.

Working with Manpower I once found myself driving a forklift.

One unforgettable job was in the sub-basement of a chemical plant. There were multi-storied vats of boiling liquid on metal lattice-work floors. Often the vats would boil over and the toxic liquid would splash through the lattice-work to collect onto the floor below. We had no idea what we had been hired to do, but as we were led to a trap door going to the sub basement we heard people exclaim, "But they're not wearing hats."

Our job was to go into the basement and with squeegee brushes, push the melange of ejected chemicals to a point where there was a sewer exit. One can only guess where it went from there.

As we made our way deep into the basement we could hear "ka-shoom!", then an onrush of liquid somewhere in the dark. Our steps, never very sure to begin with, slowed. We did push a little of the chemical mixture toward the center, but then with a "ka-shoom," a jet of chemicals splashed right behind Jay. With that he threw his squeegee away and all of us sloshed our way back to the trap door, throwing away our rubber capes and boots as we ran from the plant.

Whenever Jay became tired of a place we would pack up and move on. But we always seemed to need something that we could not afford. Jay would simply go out and write checks.

Because I thought I loved him, I joined him on his path for a time. It was during this time, by the way that I changed my name. I had been born Michael Mower but changed my name to Michael Fleming. Later, a Guru named Ma Jaya gave me the spiritual name of Brahmacharya Baba, but that's another story.

Like so many things, writing bad checks can become habit-forming; done without really thinking of the consequences both to myself and to the person or company who received the check.

Finally, there was one check that shook me back into the person that I really was and am; a person who is honest and caring. I had written a check to a man for something that I really didn't need. As I reached into my wallet for my I.D. the man said, "You don't have to show me that, I trust you."

I was sickened to realize that I had taken advantage of a person who trusted me. For years I have sent that man all the positive and helpful thoughts that I can. At night I used to visualize him with great wealth.

I was not like Jay, but bit by bit I lost myself in him. Slowly, I also lost my self-esteem—becoming totally dependent upon him as well. He really didn't care. I don't think he really cared about anything. Jay was a pushy con-artist, a liar, cheat and a thief. I was taken in by his stories and his seeming capabilities as were most people around him. I came to believe that he was more capable than me. He would lie without thinking about it. According to him, he could do, or had done, almost everything and I believed him. It is no surprise that the longer I stayed with him the less confidence I had in myself. Even meeting people became difficult for me; so much so that if a person knocked at the door, I would cringe and get Jay to answer it. Slowly, but surely, I became convinced that I was incompetent.

We lived together for several years; moving from state to state and doing odd jobs. Sometimes I would get a job as a programmer but since I had come to dislike programming, physical labor became the job of choice.

Somewhere along the way we got a Ouija board. It worked well for us, especially for Jay. Through it we met a spirit who named himself Gary. Gary said he had been gay and a body builder when living. We had many adventures with him leading us. He had us set up a gym in the basement of a house where we were living in Bountiful, Utah, prompting us to put pictures of muscle builders on the walls to inspire us. Gary even had us put on "shows," to impress our few friends. Soon, Jay put aside the Ouija board and started "automatic typing." I was so jealous. I wanted so badly to touch the other side of life. I had had a lover named Buddy in the 1960s who was a trance medium. Buddy had given me a life reading so this sort of thing was not new to me. I had always wanted to be a medium. One day during a session with Gary, I asked why Jay could contact him while I could not. The answer came back, "Because Jay doesn't give a damn."

That was a good description of Jay. He just did not give a

damn. He really didn't have any morals that I could see. He lied without thinking, took without caring, and lived without taking responsibility for himself or the damage that he did to others.

On my birthday, January 19, 1976, Jay left; again. Just like he got tired of being in one place too long, I guess he just got tired of me. He had found another person and said that he loved him. I doubt very much that he was capable of that emotion, but it was the excuse he used.

He was gone again. Jay was like that. No strings, no ties. After all we had gone through together he was still able to walk away without a second thought. I had no idea what to do, although I do know that it was the best thing that ever happened to me.

I tried to move in with my mother and stepfather in Salt Lake City. I had even moved a few boxes into the house, but the feelings from my stepfather were so hostile that I moved right back out again.

My mother had had a nervous breakdown several years earlier. She took valium several times a day and at night she took thorazine to help her sleep, (the same horse tranquilizer that had calmed me after the LSD trips).

I found a large bottle of Valium #15 that my stepfather had been stealing from my mother. As I left, I took his stolen cache figuring it would serve him right.

I moved myself out from my mothers house and into a small apartment on Main Street in Salt Lake City. Jay was gone. I used the valium that I had taken from my stepfather and soon became addicted to it. The pills made the days and nights bearable for me. Wanting desperately to be a medium I began to do "automatic writing." Receiving writings from Mary, Joseph and Claude, who had been my dad. More and more lonely, I took more valium as well. My drug-clouded mind wrote messages that I wanted to see as I began to question the value of my life.

When I was with the hippies we would say, "We are One." If that were true, then I was the brother of Christ. Hence, I decided, I was also an embodiment of the savior and I needed to die. Slowly it began to unfold in my mind that I was to take my life. I did not want someone to have to do it for me. I would do it myself. Therefore, there would be no sin for anyone else. Jesus needed the help of the Jews but I would take care of it myself, so there could be no blame to anyone else. My writings concurred that I should do this.

Standing in a crowded bar one evening, the bartender kept passing me by as if I was invisible. I figured that I was already gone and only awaiting the act to finish the deed.

The night was snowy. I was coming back to the apartment when my truck died in the middle of Main Street, Salt Lake City, right in front of my apartment building. I just left it where it was and went inside. Tonight was to be the night. Over the past few days I had written a poem about it:

Last moment before the dawn.

The die is cast and games go on.
Let go the past, here comes the dawn,
The new day dawns with purest light,
born from depths of darkest night.

How comes this day born out of lies
let loosed at last from by-gone ties?
If truth be known, like each new breath
new life is born from naught but death.

Surely the agony of waiting lies deeper
than pain's reality.
"It doesn't matter now."

The words, though delivered in passion and anger
- - have brought a kind of peace.

Through the stillness of the night the echo of my own voice
comes back to me:
- - would that I had spoken the truth.

And now, alone, even dreams do not my stillness break.
And the spirits have been silenced as with friends.
What now shall I speak?
Or shall I be silent even from myself?

The stillness of the night hangs so close
I dare not even think,
lest the calmness of the moment pass me by.

No longing stirs my inner soul.
My heart, not fouled by need or goal.
"I am," I thought, which will suffice.
I will not need to waken twice.

And now I walk alone within myself, feeling myself
and finding myself discovering that which "I am."

And I can say that the decision is my own.
For none can enter in to influence nor sway me in my resolve.

Be quick, oh scythe in Reapers hand to cut this shaft of grain.
The time is right for harvest now and will not be again.

What is death, but the fulfillment of life?

It well may be that I shall never touch another body.
Ah, but I have touched many.

Have my teeth fixed; "Ha,"
What I must chew confounds the surest of teeth.

And I stabbed myself. It wasn't dramatic at all. I just pushed a butcher knife into my stomach. To my amazement, nothing happened. I was standing there holding the knife which was sticking out of my stomach. "Is this deep enough?" I wrote, holding the knife in my stomach with one hand while wrote. "Yes," came the answer, so I laid down and prepared to die. I had expected something to happen, but it didn't.

Morning came to find me on the bed, quite alive, but with a piece of my stomach hanging out about two inches and the knife laying beside me. I put a bandage over the protruding wound and began to wonder what to do since I was still alive.

Jay happened to find me and hour or so later; he had seen and recognized my truck in the middle of the Street and had gone looking for me. He found me with a bandage barely covering the protruding fat or whatever it was that was sticking out.

I was still not quite sure why I was still alive.

Not wanting to be bothered with me, Jay put me on a bus for Los Angeles. I was met by my friend, Little Mike. I could always count on Mike. When I gave everything away to become a hippie he took my coffee table and stored it in his garage to await the day when I would "come to my senses." I have it to this day. He also took in Lous and Lewis from Rotterdam when they came to visit me, but found that I was on some kind of spree with Jay. Mike met me at the bus station and took me to lunch. Part way through the meal I said, "I think I need to go to the hospital."

I was in a line with many other emergency patents at L.A. County General Hospital. A teacher/doctor finally came by checking on all of us. He saw my stomach and yelled, "Get this guy into surgery NOW!" Two student surgeons worked on me. They had no assistants, but I trusted them. At one point I said, "I think I'm going to faint." I was hyperventilating. "Could I please have a wet towel?" Of course, neither of them could leave, so they yelled out the door to the students passing by. But it was time to change shifts and no one wanted to stop.

Finally, they got the attention of one of the student nurses who was leaving. "He's hyperventilating. Please put a cold towel on his head," one of the student doctors said. She went to the sink with a towel and filled it with water. She did not wring it out but came back, and holding it about a foot over my face, she let it drop. For a person who was wanting to learn to heal, she didn't seem to feel any compassion. "Did you see that?" One of the student doctors asked, "Sure did," the other replied.

Then it was done. The surgery was over, and I was left alone. Of course it was time for a shift change. (Perhaps I'm lucky that they actually stayed to finished the stitches.) I was lying in a pool of blood, sweat and water from the wet towel. No one was near so I got out of bed and looked in the cupboards. I found some sheets and changed them so I could be dry.

When I did get moved out of the emergency ward, things got a lot better. The nurse even got me some cigarettes. I was addicted to them at that time. My mind was still a problem, however. I had fallen apart again after the suicide attempt, and had a mental breakdown.

My friend Marshall, who had taken care of me when I had freaked out on acid trips, was taking care of me yet again. Gently and slowly he was helping me to gain back my confidence, independence, and self-reliance. God bless him. Friends like Marshall and Mike are priceless.

In my attempted suicide, I cleared up a deeply felt doubt that I had held about myself; about how far I would go to help to save the world if need be. This doubt had its roots during the time when I was taking the acid trips in the late 1960s before I gave the house away. I was shaken out of a deep sleep by a violent earthquake. As I awakened, I had the overwhelming feeling that I had the power to stop the quake and the resulting destruction if only I would allow myself to die.

Leaping from my bed, I began to spread my arms out to embrace death. But I had a thought that if I died, I would not be able to help or teach (or something like that). A few seconds' hesitation and the moment passed me by. It was too late; the moment's thought was gone and I was left wondering what I might have done. After a short time, I realized that I did not have the wisdom necessary to stop the world from doing what it needed to do to relieve its pent-up stress. I allowed myself to accept this thought, but the doubt had lingered within my mind. Now as I was recovering from the stab wound, I knew at last that I would indeed sacrifice my life for the world if it was necessary.

Months had passed. I had a job programming again at Occidental Life Insurance Company. Like it or not, programming was a way to make money. I was getting back on my feet and had bought myself a motorcycle. The motorcycle was significant because it represented a change in the way I had begun to think about me; a change that imbued independence and freedom. Slowly I was creating a new life for myself.

At that time, I was also learning to read the "New Tarot." Still very much a loner, I spent most of my time by myself in my bedroom. The Tarot cards became alive for me. Several times each day, I would read for myself. In many ways, The Tarot became my friend. I would ask questions about my mental stability. One time I read it and interpreted it to read, " Yes you're crazy, but you're getting better." Other than spending limited time with Marshall in the evenings, I would shut myself up with the Tarot, and as a result I learned to read it very well. I've even collected my own writings and thoughts into a book to be called, *The New Tarot of ONE*, which is centered on a card that I have designed called: *The ONE card*.

One day, I felt an urgent need to read the Tarot. I could feel that something was happening. I felt the power of the cards as I laid them out. The energy was palpable. I was so close to the cards that I was able to read in them that Jay would call me that day. I was totally shaken. I had not heard anything from Jay since he put me on the bus in Salt Lake City months ago. I thought I was over him, that he no longer affected me. Yet, I was literally shaking as I waited for the call to come. And Jay did call. He said he wanted to get together with me that night.

So many thoughts went through my mind: mostly thoughts of expectation, though I couldn't have said what it was that I expected. As I drove my motorcycle over to meet Jay, I was filled with excitement. I wanted him to see that I was driving a motorcycle, something I had never done before. It exemplified the independence and freedom that I was creating for myself. I also wanted to tell him of my new job and the Tarot, and of all the things that had been happening with me.

Jay was not alone. He wanted to show off his new date.

There was very little talking and no "catching up." It was so like Jay to be careless of my feelings, and so like me not to have expected it. I didn't let him know of my disappointment and we all decided to meet at a local bar. I led the way on my motorcycle, (as I remember, he made a point of not mentioning it). My mind was trying to make sense of it all. Jay, as usual, had been able to walk into my life, disrupt it, and walk all over my feelings without any sentiment at all on his part.

We were stopped at a streetlight and needed to make a left hand turn. The light turned green. I thought it was a "left arrow" light and I drove into the intersection to make a left hand turn. It wasn't a left arrow light, however. It was a green light and a truck was coming directly at me from the opposite direction. We were heading toward each other at a fairly rapid speed. Disaster was impending. Startled by the oncoming truck, I jumped, but my left hand kept hold of the handlebar (the one which regulates the gas). My hand twisted on the gas as I jumped, making the motorcycle surge forth in a burst of power that literally caused my body to become airborne; flying behind the motorcycle while holding desperately to the gas handle.

What a picture that must have been! Without any direction from me, the motorcycle went alongside the truck, then behind it and in front of a car that was following. I was holding onto the handlebar, flying right behind. As if following a script the motorcycle came to a stop at the curb, just out of the intersection. I fell back into the seat feet first, holding onto the motorcycle, with everything under control.

I seemed under control as well, but inside I was stunned to say the least. Jay and his friend came running up to me with white faces. I forgot what they said. It really didn't matter to me. They were in shock. I suspect I acted as if it was an ordinary day's experience. And somehow, Jay really didn't matter to me any more.

We went on to the bar and the evening progressed. My eyes were finally opened to Jay. It was later that night when I was in bed before sleep that I recalled the events of the evening. I saw the motorcycle hit the truck and my body splat against the truck face. I could even feel the transition of the spirit. The events were too unconventional to ignore. Why was I not dead (again)?

Then I realized that I've done some extraordinary things in this life. I've experienced events that I have called "miracles" (this story is one of them). I do believe that we create our own lives. We are not victims, and I know that I have something to say. If I were to have died in either of these events, my stories would not have been told. I feel that a higher part of myself did not want to waste the events of this living, and simply created a different reality for me to live out. A different pathway as it were.

I have to find something positive to say about the part of my life that I shared with Jay. In searching my mind I realize that before becoming a hippie, I felt that I was better than other people. Growing up in a Mormon family in the Mormon Church, with their belief that they are the only true church, certainly helped with that opinion. Then again, my own ego heaped on the "better than" attitude.

After the time with Jay I could no longer say or think that I am any better than anyone else. I have never forgotten that lesson.

As I look back while writing these stories I realize that I have lived many lives in this Living.

> The intensity is all important. If you have, for example, a highly vivid desire to be somewhere else, then without realizing it consciously a pseudo physical form, identical with your own, may appear in that very spot. The desire will carry the imprint of your personality and image.
> Seth Speaks by Jane Roberts

Chapter 7

Psychic

I was finding my way back to sanity. Marshall had taken care of me yet again. I was finally free of Jay and his negativity. Now I was to enter a time of many physical problems which would lead me into another life: a time of physical pain but spiritual growth. It seems that I had indeed gone from one life to another with my wild motorcycle ride.

Once I had recovered and was working steadily again, my friend John Keel, invited me to move in with him. John lived on a hill in Silverlake, just above the house that I had given away.

Years earlier, when I was still living down the hill, John had wanted to make an astrology chart for me. He was an excellent astrologer. When he asked me what time I was born, I answered, "10:30 P.M." He said, "No one is born at 10:30, they are born at ten thirty-five perhaps, but not right on the hour or half hour." Then he asked me to tell him dates of major events that had happened in my life. I told him the date of the death of my father and other things that I could remember. He said that he would do what is called a "chart rectification." A few days later, John had a chart for me. "You weren't born at 10:30," he told me. "You were born at 10:45." I got a passport several years later and needed my birth certificate. Sure enough, John was right. I was born at 10:45.

He then proceeded to read for me. He was accurate about several things in my chart, especially about the time of Saturn's return and the major changes it would bring into my life. I had entered this time of change with the acid trips and the hippies. His statement that I would probably form my own religion was also coming true. My visions had led me away from established religion. The supernatural experiences that I was actually living were giving me insight into deeper meanings of reality and I was very much creating my own philosophy and my own religion, if only for myself.

I stayed with John in his house for a month or so. One day he told me that he thought I should have my own space. He had a small apartment in the lower part of his house and wanted me to move there. He said that I should surround myself with the things that I had of my own, and say, "Mine." John was a very wise man in many ways. I did indeed need to be alone in a space that I could consider "mine," and with things that I could call my own. After giving everything away, it was time for me to understand that it was okay to have possessions again.

It was going to be very exciting living alone; really alone for the first time in my life. Basically I was just moving downstairs, but it was my own space. I was carrying a large potted plant down the back stairs when a step broke beneath me. I fell and lost control of the plant which landed in my crotch. Soon I was in bed with epididymitis, an infection of a testicle. At times the pain was almost unbearable. I was out from work for a few days but when I came back to work my crotch was so swollen that I looked like some of the football players; all padded and protected. One of the secretaries even swooned.

My urologist said that we were going to have to remove the testicle and made an appointment for me to enter the hospital for the procedure. I continued to work while awaiting the surgery.

Working as a programmer at Occidental Life Insurance Company, I had made several programmer friendships. One of them--yet another John. John Coffey became a close friend whose friendship I enjoy to this day. One day when John and I were leaving work, we noticed a sign saying, "Free swine flu shots." John suggested that we get the shot. The sign said that there had been warnings that the swine flu would be coming and would be very bad this year, so I said, "Why not?"

Soon, I not only had a swollen crotch, but I was getting weaker. Each day I could feel that my body had to fight more just to walk. I went to the company nurse. I was to enter the hospital the following day to have the testicle removed. The nurse advised me to say nothing about the sudden weakness until I had gone into the hospital. "Then they will have to keep you until they figure out what the weakness is all about," she continued.

I had to take a bus to get to the hospital. I remember sliding the small suitcase out of the bus and dragging it down the stairway. Strength was quickly leaving my body. I was so weak I could not lift the small bag, so I had to drag and push it on the walkway and up the stairs into the hospital.

The next morning I awoke to find many bandages around my crotch. It seems that the testicle had grown so large it had attached itself to the sac, called "Granulomitis, Orchitis." I was paralyzed as well; I had Guillian Barre Syndrome, (French polio).

I had to go to the bathroom about that time, and they gave me a bed pan. "No," I told them. "I'll walk to the bathroom myself," and I did. I absolutely refused to be paralyzed.

Somehow Jay had found out that I was in the hospital and came to visit me. The T.V. was on and a newscaster was reporting that there was a flu outbreak called Guillian Barre Syndrome and that several people had already died of the disease. Jay's face went white and he shook. It was the only time I ever saw him react with any feeling.

When they released me, they told me that I would be in various stages of paralysis for about a year. In that time I was not to tire any muscles. "Use it and loose it," they said. Whatever I did, I was not to let any muscles get tired out or they would stay that way. When I left the hospital, the first thing I did was to climb a cliff.

It was in Griffith Park, a place where I spent some time almost every day. The cliff I was to climb was about sixty feet high and fairly steep. It was at the end of a gentle walk from the road where I parked my car. Slowly, I walked into the park. I walked a few steps then sat down on a fallen tree for a bit. After that, I would walk a few steps more and rest again. When I got to the base of the cliff I climbed a step up then rested. I was on disability so I had all the time I needed. Slowly, one step at a time, I climbed the cliff without tiring.

I wrote to my stepmother during that time to tell her of my condition. My hand could hardly hold the pen and the letters were so large they filled several pages with just a few words. "I'm paralyzed," I wrote. When an answering letter arrived my stepmother didn't even mention my paralysis, writing only about her own world and her own pains. It seemed that neither my mother nor my step mother cared very much about me.

There wasn't too much for me to do except walk slowly in the park or relax. I continued to work with the Tarot cards and I read quite a variety of spiritual books during that time as well. I had several very vivid dreams, most I could not remember, but there was a recurring theme: A symbol resembling two intercrossed figure eights.

In one dream there was a lamp post with four lights on top. A lighted "electron" was swiftly circling a light bulb. It would encircle the bulb once, then traverse the circle moving to the next bulb and encircle it as well; continuing around and through the four bulbs in a continuous motion.

Another dream showed a ride that we have in local fairs called a "Tilt-a-whirl." Rounded seats revolve around in a circle. They are, in turn, set upon a circling base that itself is revolving. The doubled eight was obvious in that dream as well. I took this to be my own symbol and have used it as such ever since. This is my symbol:

One day, there appeared in my mind a very buxom and matronly woman. I could see her standing at one end of my kitchen, arms folded under her ample breasts. She was going to teach me to cook. Among other things, she taught me to make three-tiered vegetables and a cheap thick roast beef cooked to perfection. She also taught me to use a steamer instead of boiling vegetables. Ahhhh, such a difference!

I don't remember much more about what she taught me, but I do remember her presence about me many times. Each time she was helping me to learn new things. I was so pleased to have her there. There were never words. She did not speak. She was just there, and I knew what she wanted me to do.

There was a time during my recovery when I patronized a local bar called "Woody's Hyperion." It was a very popular place to socialize in the afternoons and early evening. I fell in with a group of ex-hippies and other spiritual people. The conversation would always drift toward subjects of a spiritual nature. We were reading "*Sand and Foam*" by Kahlil Gibran, discussing his aphorisms over our beers and games of pool. We were discovering Spiritualism; talking about other dimensions or things like that while drinking beer at a bar. What an unusual, but fun combination. I enjoyed going there very much.

One day a good looking guy came into the bar. There were only a few of us there so he and I chatted awhile. I didn't think he would be interested in me so I told him that if he waited, there were many good looking guys coming later. "What's wrong with what I've got?" he said. We dated several times after that. He tried to get me to quit smoking but I resisted; I suspect that was the reason we eventually went our separate ways, but it was very nice while it lasted.

There was a very beautifully landscaped yard behind my apartment. My kitchen opened up on it. Often we would walk naked among the profuse plants and trees and we spent many wonderful afternoons lazing among the beauty. One afternoon I went into the yard and realized that there was a tree stump that I had never really noticed before. I wondered what the tree had looked like before it had been cut down; but then, I think this poem tells it best.

July 19, 1976

>The man came into the garden and shared its life. He saw a tree with a healed part where a limb had been cut away. He placed his hand there to bless, and to know,
>
>- - And the man felt the pulse of the tree.
>
>Looking closer into the fertile and moss covered ground, the man saw all manner of things expressing their livingness.
>
>His gaze came upon an ant running back and forth and over and under a leaf. The stem of the leaf was surrounded with a web where a spider was waiting patiently. The ant ran again under the leaf and back up onto the top looking for a way off of the leaf to safety.
>
>Raising his hand, the man stretched forth his finger just below the leaf and the ant jumped onto his fingernail. He lowered his hand and as the ant jumped free, running into the grass;,
>
>and the man felt the pulse of God.

During this time I went through a spiritual revolution or rebirth - not all at once, but at different times and different places. I remember receiving the name Many Feathers during a re-birthing session. I was also given the name Brahmacharya Baba by a guru named Ma Jaya Sati Bagavati. She told me that she had been inspired to give me the name and that it meant celibacy: She wanted me to be celibate but I rebelled. I really didn't want a guru by then anyway, but I did enjoy the company of spiritual people. I found that the name Brahmacharya also means, "One who walks in the pathway of God." Baba means Teacher or Father. I preferred these meanings.

I had become involved with spiritualist churches as well. It was the spiritual readings that attracted me. There was one woman who got up and gave remarkable readings to people. I was one of the recipients. She said that she was going to teach Psychic classes. I was excited and I joined the class. It was great! The energy was so charged! I could feel it! Some of the things we did in class were astounding.

We wrote our names on pieces of paper, threw them into a pile, then selected one. We were to describe that person's house. "I'm going up three stairs in the middle of a building," I began. "Now I'm going down a hallway to the third door on the left. Inside, there is a room to the left. I am in the front room. Now I'm going down a hallway from the front room. I come upon two rooms." "Only one," the girl whose name I had chosen interrupted. "What is the other room?" I asked. "It's a closet," she replied. "Why are there no paintings on the walls?" I continued. "Because we are just moving in." As my mind passed the kitchen nook I exclaimed, "You hate that light fixture don't you?" "I despise it," she said.

Another time our teacher said that there was a very high spirit among us. She asked if anyone could feel it. "I can," I said. "He's right in front of me although he has no body." "Where he comes from, they need no identity," was her response.

One day she said she was going to have a séance. It would cost $15 to have a reading. Of course I went. She appeared to go into a trance state, although I really wasn't sure if she was in a trance at all. She assumed a very prissy voice. She said that she was my great-great-grandmother, who then proceeded to tell me that I should go back to my family. My great-great-grandmother came across the plains with the Mormon pioneers. She would have been a farmer's wife who worked the soil. She certainly would not have been prissy.

I had become estranged from my family and the teacher knew of the distance between us. She had used that knowledge to have my "great-great-grandmother" advise me to return to them. I knew that to give advice is one thing but to say that the advice came from a spirit when it didn't, was a different thing entirely. I left knowing that both her and the reading had been fake. She had betrayed her integrity for $15.

The next day at the church I could see that she no longer had the "glow" about her that I had become familiar with. I felt that the high spirits that had been with her had abandoned her in her dishonesty. Her classes, as well, lost their energy as the spiritual teachers drifted away. I felt the loss intensely. Within a year she was to die of cancer. I learned a lot from that entire experience and have gone to extraordinary lengths ever since never to lie when giving a reading, although I sometimes say that I'm not sure about something. On occasion I have even interjected, "I think that was me who said that."

One day my bud, Little Mike and I got together. He told me that he had cancer and had only a few months to live. I was still recovering from being paralyzed and had to watch how I used my energy, but I moved in to take care of him and his mother, Anne.

One step and rest. One slow movement at a time without tiring myself, I took care of them. I practiced spirit reading with Mike. There was a time just before he died when I saw the image of a very good looking man. I knew that he would help Mike make the transition. I told Mike about him and what I thought he looked like.

Mike finally entered City of Hope, a cancer research hospital. As it turned out, Jay once again emerged into my life. He knew where I was and called to ask me to go out to dinner with him. It was the first time I would be away from the responsibilities of taking care of Mike and his mom, so I accepted. While we were at dinner, Little Mike died. He had called his house looking for me but, of course, I was out.

What was it about me that I allowed Jay to have so much control over my life? Although I had faced a lot of my past on acid, there was one more thorn was yet to pull. A thorn that had its origination at the moment of my conception: My mother did not want another child and tried to abort me.

I was very young sitting on the edge of the bathtub, taking bobby pins, one by one out of a tin box, spreading them apart on my finger and handing them to my mother as she put up her hair. "Do you know where I got that box"? she asked. When I shook my head, "no," she told me that the box had contained miscarriage pills and that she had taken them all. She would beat on her stomach, and jump off of the porch and beat her stomach again in attempt to get rid of me. "I cried when you were born," she continued, "because I wanted another girl."

She followed that story by telling me that when I was three months old, my great-uncle, who was the town doctor, happened to drop by. "Get this kid to the hospital, he's dying"! he had yelled at her. She said that I was dying of rickets complicated with malnutrition. "But when mommy saw you in the hospital with all those needles sticking in you, and your arms all swollen up, then mommy loved you."

I am convinced that my expression never changed as I spread another bobby pin, put it on the end of my finger, and handed it to her. Instead, I buried her story deep inside; to grow over the years and fester.

I was to become a hypochondriac for the first thirty years of my life. Insecure and unwanted, I began to try to buy the love of my mother and my friends.

When I moved away from home and became a programmer I masked this insecurity with an attitude that bordered on arrogance, and as has been stated before, a feeling of being better than others. Seeing through that masking, however, revealed that I still felt I had to earn love and caring from my friends.

Post-hippie I became much more loving and gentle, but while I took many leaps of faith I still felt insecure.

Jay had a strong and abusive personality that I was unconsciously drawn to. I was not his victim; I was a victim of my own deep-seated self doubt. Even when I finally pushed him out of my life I was still drawn to abusive relationships. Many years after this particular time in my life, I was again drawn into an abusive relationship. This time I turned to therapy for help and after several years I was able to finally pull that festering thorn. Happily, I no longer allow negative people into my life.

At Little Mike's funeral, I became bored. I wasn't really paying attention to the service and I decided to try to make contact with him. "Michael, Michael," I said in my mind, calling out to him. "MICHAEL!" came resounding within my brain. The feeling was my old friend saying, "Stop it!" I suppose that since it was his funeral, he was paying attention; even if I wasn't.

I continued practicing spiritual readings and studying the Tarot. I really wanted to be a channel like Jay had been. Soon I was giving readings at church. It was the same spiritualist church where I had found the teacher. Once I gave a reading to my friend, Reverend Harold. Harold had a small group of followers who gathered together each Sunday in a small building where he would conduct a service. Harold had lost the rental of the small place that he called his church and was looking for another. "You are going to get another church," I told him. Harold was so excited but as he sat down, I pointed to him and said, "but this will not be YOUR church." He did get a church a few weeks later. Only a few months later, he lost it.

It was during this time that I gave a speech at The Thomas Institute of Metaphysics in Los Angeles. The talk described an essence of God. From my own experience; I had learned that one cannot know God without a thorough and honest knowledge of one's self; therefore the talk was titled,

"*Who am I.*" Most of my talk consisted of the things that my old friends, after my acid trips, simply did not want to hear. With this audience however, it was very well received.

Soon thereafter, Little Mike's mother, Anne died. She was bitter to the end saying that there is no greater curse than to have outlived both of her sons. Mothers around the globe I'm sure, agree with her. Some years earlier, she told me how she got her name. Her mother had decided on her name but the village priest (in Ireland) said, "You'll be doing no such thing. You'll name her after our blessed virgin." Her mother stood her ground and insisted. Nonetheless at the naming ceremony, the priest gave her the name that he wanted her to have, Anne Mary. She told me she hated this priest and would curse him until her dying day. I tried to tell her that she was the only one she was hurting, but she didn't listen. Bitter to the end, she carried her curse with her to her grave.

After Anne died, I moved back to my apartment beneath John's house.

I was going out on my motorcycle at one point when Jay appeared at the end of the driveway. "I'm moving to -- " (I can't remember where because I really wasn't listening). "Really," I replied. "Don't you want to know my address?" he whined. "Absolutely not," I countered. And with a quick twist to the gas handle I sped off, leaving Jay (hopefully) standing in the dust.

Little Mike was gone, Anne was gone, Jay was gone. The hippie days were passing away, and I was recovering from paralysis. Another life was ending for me and another was awaiting.

Recipes given to me by the buxom lady spirit:

Three tiered steamed vegetables

Note: When cutting the vegetables do not cut them too small or they may get overcooked.

1 - Begin with chopped green beans, carrots, brussel sprouts or other hard vegetables. Place them in a steamer, cover and bring to a steam. Turn off the heat but do not lift the lid.
Wait 3 to 5 minutes letting the steam do the work.

2 - Add chopped potatoes, celery, onion, broccoli, cauliflower or other medium hard vegetables. Even uncooked pasta.
Also at this time add whatever spices or herbs you like.
Bring to a steam and again, turn off the heat and do not lift the lid.

3 - After about 5 minutes add chopped zucchini, cabbage or other soft vegetables.
Bring to a steam again, turn off the heat and let it set for a short time.

Then test to see if they are done enough. If not, just bring them to a steam one more time and again, do not lift the lid.

When finished toss with butter and serve. It's wonderful and it's easy. Other than turning off when the heat steam begins to show,
the timing is very flexible and forgiving.

Broiled roast beef
(With Apologies to my vegetarian friends)

For a roast I used to use about a 1 1/2" wide chuck or seven bone roast. Season both sides of the roast with spices and herbs that you like. (I also like to add some soy sauce). Rub in the spices so they adhere evenly. Turn the oven on to broil and preheat. Cut an onion into slices about 3/8" thick and separate into rings. Place half of the sliced onions separately on top of the roast. Put under the broiler as close to the heat as possible. Broil until the onions are burnt. Turn the roast over, add more sliced onions and again broil until the onions are burnt. The roast always comes out perfectly, unless you like it blood rare or cooked to death.

Chapter 8

Break an Arm and Find a New Life

Loosing my best friend was a blow to me. After Little Mike died I moved into an apartment with Kent, a friend of mine from work. I was a programmer again. Kent had AIDS and was also to die within a year. I tried to help him prepare for leaving this life. Yet, in his last few days, he sat on the couch with his hands clenched into fists. Holding onto the life that was leaving his body.

Great changes were about to happen.

I was walking down a lane in Elizabethan England around the year 1578. All around me were peasants, nobles, shopkeepers and a variety of other people living their lives. There were more than 1200 performers living the life of their Renaissance characters and wearing totally realistic costumes that they had made themselves. Their roles were improvisational, meaning that they reacted to each other much as we would in real life. They also reacted to and with me.

The sounds, the smells, the sights, the shops, the costumes, the actors and the food combined so realistically that it seemed like I was walking through a faire in rural England during the reign of Queen Elizabeth I. I was walking through time with my friend, Kent. There was no fast food, no mass produced items for sale, everything was made by hand. There was beer however, and throughout the day I had consumed my share of the dark beverage. They were really living what I was seeing, creating a "living history" of daily life unfolding in a small Elizabethan town faire. I was surrounded by this wonderful "happening."

Pointing my finger all around me I said, "I'm going to work in this faire." I had consumed perhaps too many beers, for at that point I fell forward to the ground and hit my head upon a rock. Blood coming from the wound did not stop me. I put some wet paper on my forehead and stayed until the closing of the faire forced us to leave.

The following day at work, I told my fellow programmers about the faire and that I planned to work in it the following year if I could only figure out how to do it. My friend, John Coffey grinned, "Bruce, upstairs on the third floor, plays Lord Derby at the faire. Come on, I'll introduce you." That's all it took. Before long I was taking part in rehearsals for the next faire. I became Michael Fleming, valet and later steward to the Earl of Derby. As you can see by the name of my character I did not use much imagination at this point in my life. Michael Fleming was just me, in olden times and in a costume. It turns out that I was a very good actor though, and I ended up getting some excellent parts. I loved acting, and I loved the Renaissance faire.

MF/BB

Looking back, I realize that I had started acting when I was a child. I used to put on plays using my playmates as actors in my performances. Sheets hanging from clotheslines served as our curtains. I would write the scripts and make the costumes myself. I used to love making paper crowns with little jewels that I glued on. My plays always had a King (a role that somehow I always managed to play). The Buddy and Mike show eight years earlier had also whetted my appetite for performing.

Acting in the Renaissance faire had a very profound affect on my life. As an improvisational actor, I was able to express myself in many ways that Michael Fleming, the programmer, would never have dared. The character did things that the actor himself wouldn't have dreamed of doing.

Michael the valet was a nondescript kind of character at first, so I began to challenge myself in the role; trying out new things and testing my limits. This growth in my acting also reflected upon my personal life. Michael Fleming, the programmer, began testing and stretching limits as well. I learned to say "No," to have opinions and desires. This was new to me as a person.

I was and still am shy in many ways. On stage, however, or in front of a group, the acting "persona" takes over and it's like I become someone else. The shyness is gone and a very assertive and expressive guy takes over. It is as if I transform into another person. It is that persona that has helped me to grow several times.

After a few years, I found myself bored with the character that I had created. I wanted to increase and challenge my role (and my life), so I created a character that would really challenge me; "Styx."

"Styx, be I, light o' finger and heavy o' fist and foot, I be." Byron Sticks, actually, was to be a daring, dashing, cunning and romantic, thief. Creating Styx was indeed a challenge for me. The time I spent with Jay aside, I certainly am not a thief and I don't do well at telling lies either. I didn't know much about Styx. At first Styx was just the costume that I was making: used leather made a authentic looking codpiece and vest. I then made a hat designed from a picture that I had seen in a book on Elizabeth I.

I figured that I would find Styx's personality by wearing his costume and interacting with other actors.

Later I was to create another character named Philpot Styx who was Byron's uncle. Philpot was a successful fish merchant who despised poor Byron.

April 29, 1978 was opening day of the faire and I was about to introduce Styx. As the debut for my new character, I was to steal a goblet from a noble at court. My friend, Dawn played the Countess Northumberland. It was her goblet that I was to steal and thus introduce "Styx, the great and renowned thief."

The nobles were waiting for the Queen to appear. There I was, easing my way slowly toward the Countess. "Man! You there!" The countess was pointing at me. Making a slight and sloppy bow, I approached her. "Hold this," she said as she held out her goblet to me. Flashing a conspiratorial look at the audience gathered about, I gently slipped the goblet inside my shirt and slowly began to back away into the gathered crowd. "Guards, stop that man!" she yelled, and five of the Queen's guards started running toward me. I had not expected this reaction. I really hadn't planned for any reaction at all, but there I was running with the guards chasing right behind. And I ran directly over the side of a sloped cliff about 40 feet high.

Flying through the air, face downward, time seemed unhurried as I watched the goblet rise up out of my shirt and slowly fly away. (We were never able to find it.) My slow motion flight came to an abrupt end as I landed on my right elbow. I heard a cracking sound and knew that I had broken my arm. I could see several of the guards running down the hill after me. (They had the good sense to run down the hill instead of trying to fly.) Using my forward motion, I came to my feet and started to run again. I ran limp-armed through the faire with the guards in hot pursuit.

It must have been quite a sight for the audience to see me falling down the cliff with the guards chasing me. They were probably wondering how we had rehearsed such an act to make it work and make it seem so real. My arm just hung there but everything else was working perfectly so I ran off into the crowd.

"Backstage" was right in front of me, an area curtained off for the actors to retire, relax, and refresh themselves. I could feel one of the guard's hands touching me so I dove through the curtains. "Caught you," the guard yelled also diving through the air and grabbing my legs. "No you didn't, I'm safe," I yelled back as we both skidded to a stop behind the curtains (I made sure to land on my "non hurt" side).

I lay on the ground panting for a few minutes, then got up. "I think I broke my arm," I said. As it turned out, the end of one of my arm bones, called a radial head, had broken completely off and was sticking out of my arm. The doctor simply pulled it the rest of the way out and put my arm in a cast. After a few days I returned to the doctor who removed the cast. "I'm amazed," I told him, "it hasn't hurt a bit." "It will now," the doctor said as he released my arm and let it fall to my side.

Pain such as I had never felt before shot through my arm and I screamed in agony. The doctor then moved my arm back to my side and put it into a sling and the pain went away. The pain that I had felt was the sharp edges of the broken bone as it tore at the tender flesh surrounding it. Since there were no bones to knit back together I did not have to have a cast, just to wear my arm in a sling.

"You must work at the edges of the bone until they are smooth," he told me. "Move your arm back and forth across the positions where it hurts, and continue to move it back and forth until it stops hurting; the more you make it hurt now, the less it will hurt later in your life." The doctor then put me on disability for three months so I didn't have to go back to work.

The faire was still my main consideration. Beginning the previous January I had joined with some fellow actors who had written a skit: two groups of supposed enemies would converge at a large area near the center of the faire site, and begin quarreling with each other until it ended up in a sword fight. For five months we practiced the scene and the sword fight choreography.

As luck would have it, it was my sword fighting arm that had been broken, and since I broke it on opening day, I was not going to be able to fight. Of course, my partner wasn't able to do the fight scene either. This, I think, bothered me most of all. I felt sad for both of us; we had both worked so very hard on our routine.

They had to quickly re-write our fight scene in order to deal with the missing character the first day. Later the scene was re-written to account for the fact that my character would not (could not) fight. It was my character Michael the valet, who was going to fight. I returned to the faire the day after the accident and we put my arm in a sling made of canvas. As long as my arm stayed in one position I did not feel pain so I was able to continue to act. The faire was only open on weekends, so I only had to wear the sling for one day.

I practiced moving my arm all week. The first position I worked on was straight down at my side. Gently and slowly I worked my arm back and forth until I could let it hang at my side and bring it back up into "sling position" without pain. By the following weekend's performance I was able to act as if there was nothing wrong as long as I didn't move my arm in any un-smoothed directions. One move of my arm in a direction that I had not previously smoothed, however, would cause me to scream out in pain.

I didn't miss a faire performance after the first day though, and after the first week I was able to act without the sling. Mostly I just kept my arm at my side except for a few rehearsed movements where I had smoothed the bone in limited pathways.

In the weeks before the faire opened we rehearsed the fight on the faire site. We had our own fans among our fellow actors who would come watch us as we practiced with our swords. After our first performance, where my partner, Don and I were not able to join in the fight, one of the actresses came up to me with sympathy. She knew how hurt I was at not being able to do the fight and was giving me strength and love. "I will do the sword fight before the last day of the faire," I told her. That gave me five weeks to wear the pain away.

The next day, Don and I began the painful and exacting routine of practicing our sword fight choreography. I had to smooth the edges of the broken bone so that I could move my arm in the sequence of movements choreographed for our routine. Slowly, inch by painful inch, we worked at the movements of the scripted fight. Back and forth, back and forth we worked on one movement until the pain went away. Then we continued through the routine smoothing a pathway for the sword arm to travel.

Every false move caused me to scream out in pain as a new, sharp section of the bone rubbed against already sore flesh. Some days we added just a few inches or so to the sequence, but they always added to the ones that we had smoothed the day before, and slowly but surely, the full choreography began again to unfold.

The power of positive thinking combined with the power of purposeful action allowed me to do the entire sword fight. It was the closing weekend of the faire. The director Cory would not allow us to fight before the final day. Don and I were ecstatic as we performed the sword fight on the last day of the faire, and it went perfectly.

I went through all the moves of the fight precisely. There was no pain nor shouts of hurt. I had to be very careful and exacting in my movements, but we had rehearsed the fight to perfection.

All of our actor friends were there to see the fight as it was written. I was so happy and proud for my partner who was able to show off his own sword fighting prowess. Our fans were finally treated to the full performance. What an ending to the faire, and the beginning of yet another new life for me.

The faire was over and I was left with two months to do nothing but heal my arm. Moving my arm back and forth over the places where it hurt, smoothing the sharp edges of the bone and toughening the tissue around it was to be my task for the next three months.

Since I was on disability I spent my days walking deep into Griffith Park, a mountainous area in the middle of Los Angeles, and one of the largest city parks in the world. Without it, I doubt that I would have stayed in Los Angeles. I needed to get away from the rush of the city. As I walked in the park each day, I exercised my arm, slowly moving it back and forth working and twisting it through the pain to wear another edge of the bone into smoothness.

It also brought a new awareness of nature into my life. I had been reading Carlos Castaneda's books about his adventures with his spiritual teacher, Don Juan. They dealt with the unseen worlds that exist outside of our ordinary vision in Nature. I loved the books. They gave words to the feelings that had grown within me since the time I was a hippie. In the books, Don Juan teaches Castaneda to observe, feel and interact with forces of the earth that surround him and I began to practice some of the techniques as I walked in the park.

While walking one morning, I became aware of what Don Juan had called a "power spot." It was across the hills toward Silverlake, the area of Los Angeles where I used to live before I gave the house away. I looked around to see if anyone was walking nearby. No one was there, so I stretched out my arms toward the power. I did a kind of "half-bow" in recognition. As I did, I felt an energy come up through my feet and out through my outstretched arms toward the power spot below. I heard some people coming up the road so I stopped playing with the energy and continued my walk and my exercise.

From that day on, each morning as I walked in the park, I would reach out and exchange energy with the power spot. After that I would walk on, working my arm. It was also while walking in the park that I began working with light. I was playing with energy and found that I could "splash" with my fingertips onto the top of my head. The top of my head would "open" and energy, in the form of light, would shine into my head. I also learned that if I "splashed" my fingertips onto the third eye area of the forehead, an opening would appear and the light would shine out.

I would stand in the sun, lightly brush the top of my head with my fingertips with an "opening" motion, and allow light to enter into the top of my head. Lightly brushing the area of the "third eye," the light would shine out. I could feel the light as it entered, then left, through the "openings" in my head. I worked with this energy everyday. Later, I was to put this technique into practice with incredible results.

There was a day when I was walking on a path in the park and came upon a large snake lying stretched out, sunning itself in peace across the pathway. It was about four feet long and perhaps two to three inches in diameter. Don Juan would have pointed out to Carlos Castaneda that the snake was part of his world and would have directed him to interact with it. Using my supposed example, I calmed my racing heart. *The snake does not want to harm me, and I do not wish to harm the snake*, I urged the thought. I relaxed myself so the snake would not feel threatened. Then calmly I walked forward and stepping over the snake I continued my walk with a big smile on my face. The snake just lay there and did not move.

The following day I saw the snake again stretched out across the pathway. Thinking the same thoughts as I had the day before, I calmed myself and walked toward him. As I approached, I lost my footing and fell forward. I stretched out my hand to catch myself. My hand was heading directly toward the snake. As I fell, I could see one of the snake's eyes as his sight met mine. It was as if I were looking at the pupil of his eye through a straw-like tube with a bright halo of light surrounding it. There was a sound, a very high pitched sound that seemed to carry communication to the snake. I felt as if I were being "scanned." The snake knew I meant it no harm. I caught myself just before my hand reached the snake, who, feeling or "reading" my calmness, other than looking me in the eye, did not move. Balancing myself, I stood up, stepped over the snake, and walked on. The following morning I found the snake in the road. He had been run over by a car.

That evening I had a dream where the snake came toward me.

He opened his mouth in a starfish like pattern and swallowed my arm up to the broken elbow. The snake then became an extension of my arm which I could use in my dreams. Sometimes I would play with that energy in the park by imagining a snake uncoiling from my extended arm.

After the faire closed I still wasn't working. So I found myself with little to do other than work with my arm in the park. I had about a month and a half before I needed to return to work. I had always wanted to go to Oregon. Now, with lots of time on my hands, I decided to travel. This was a trip that was to change my life..... again.

After all the work and all the practices

Michael the valet

Able to do the swordfight again

Chapter 9

Oregon

For some reason, whenever I went on a vacation I thought only of going to Salt Lake City to visit relatives. This would be one of the first times that I had gone somewhere just because I wanted to go. Following my heart was to lead me into yet another adventure; And, dare I say it? Yet another life.

Now the faire was over. I had about one and a half months of disability left before I had to go back to work. After breaking my arm at the faire, I was exploring Northern California and Oregon while recovering. Perhaps I was really looking for a home, although I really didn't think of it as such. I wasn't too happy with my life as it existed outside of the faire.

I had a sleeping bag in the back of my car, no definite plans, and unlimited places to discover. I have always loved trees but the trees in Oregon were different from any I had ever seen. Because of the large amount of rain in Oregon, the trees seemed greener and more "alive" there.

It was on this trip, that I first discovered photography and the camera. I had a Kodak Insta-matic camera; I couldn't think of a reason why I needed anything more complicated than that. Sometimes I would take many shots of the same scene. Some were close up, others farther away, and of many different angles. I figured that I would paste them together into a montage of the scene later. It was in trying to paste parts of pictures together that I finally realized that being able to control my exposure and an ability to zoom in and out would have been a big help, so I purchased an SLR camera with a zoom lens that would lead me later into a completely different career.

Back among the trees, I had a leisurely drive through Oregon. "Gas, Grass or Ass, no one rides for free." There were many bumper stickers like that. I did not have one, but that feeling was shared by most of the people who were traveling on the road at that time, including myself. Leftover hippies which I was and still am. Spiritual people looking for answers, disaffected people, Hari Krishnas and people just wandering, like me. It was a time of picking up hitchhikers and it made for interesting adventures. There were many experiences to be had by picking up a hitchhiker. People were more trusting then.

One hitchhiker I picked up told me that he lived on a farm with several artisans. They lived together in a communal situation sharing a large farm house. There was a big barn and everyone had his or her own stall where they could work on their handicrafts. Each weekend they opened the barn to tourists who bought their wares. He learned that I had a passion for building with wood and suggested that I might like to join their community. I could do my woodwork to make a living. That sounded good to me. "Who owns the farm?" I asked him. He told me that it was owned by a Christian group of some sort. "No, that won't work for me, I could never work for a religious group," I told him. "You don't have to join the church," he said, "all you have to do is go to church on Sunday." I told him that it sounded like hypocrisy to me to follow such a practice without belief.

"But you believe Jesus is your savior, don't you? Don't you believe he died for your sins"?

"No!" I exploded without thinking, "I do not believe that Jesus died for my sins. I haven't been that bad; I will pay for my own sins thank you very much. Jesus is my brother, not my savior."

In the silence that followed I realized that I had just given words to what I really had come to believe. I stand on my own two feet and take responsibility for my own actions. I am, as we all are, holy sparks from the same source. No one is better, nor worse, than any other. I thought of Jesus and other masters as older brothers perhaps, but I don't need a savior to save me, nor come between me and my God.

I let the hitch hiker out and continued on my way having gained a greater insight into myself.

Then I met Gar. He was just hitchhiking around, so we spent a few days together driving deeper into Oregon. One evening we took a side road to find a place to sleep. We laid out our sleeping bags and he showed me that peeing at the four corners of our sleeping area would mark our space for creatures that might come upon us in the night. If an animal smelled the scent of another marking its territory it would most likely avoid that area. How very natural, very much in line with what I had been reading in the stories of Don Juan by Carlos Castaneda.

Before we parted, Gar told me about a gathering that was to take place in the mountains near Eugene, Oregon in July. This was the first part of June. Gar told me that people would be coming from all over the world. People of all descriptions and all ways of life would be there, also traveling people, and hitch hikers were coming. It was called the Rainbow Gathering.

Gar also mentioned that there were some in the Rainbow Family who wanted to found a permanent home in the mountains, where they could all live communally together. I was immediately interested with the idea of joining this "family." He gave me a map and we parted. That day I headed back toward Los Angeles, planning to return in July to join the Rainbow Gathering.

It was a long way home. To ease the drive I smoked some marijuana. I drove slowly, enjoying the scenery. The 18 wheelers that passed me only wanted to be on their way. Truck drivers, wanting to speed into the night, flashed their lights showing me they wanted to pass. I wanted to drive slow so I would pull off of to the side of the road and slow down to let them pass. I did this several times with many trucks. Also I suspect that one of the truck drivers saw me smoking. Gently and slowly, I was making my way home.

"Breaker, breaker," I could almost hear the truck drivers talk about me on their radios as they passed, "Stoned hippie ahead." The truck drivers seemed to like me. I wasn't in their way and they were enjoying me pulling off the road and stopping for them. I knew they were talking about me.

Then I noticed two trucks that had already passed me slow down and let me get ahead of them. They were in the fast lane and trucks do not slow down in the fast lane; this I did notice. When both trucks were in back of me I began to feel the pressure of the powerful engines revving up the power to pass. There was a flashing of lights, "Let me pass." A truck was coming right at me. I pulled immediately to the right, but as he was passing me, the second truck passed him on the inside lane, and two huge semi trucks sped passed me at the same time. The energy of the trucks was doubled and, of course, I was stoned. The intense energy of these two trucks as they passed in tandem echoed within my brain. What a profound experience that was! I flashed my lights and jumped for joy. Truckers can be fun if you respect them.

It was late and I needed a cup of coffee. I saw a little cafe beside the road and I pulled over. There were a few tables with families eating together enjoying a gentle evening out. I sat at the counter. The full figured waitress paid little attention to me. It was late and she was tired, probably ready to go home. She did manage to get me a cup of coffee, however reluctantly. A few minutes later she leaned her elbows on the counter to relax. As she did, I happened to notice that there was a button unbuttoned on her blouse and I could see her breasts rub together as she moved. She saw that I noticed this and immediately paid attention to me. She gave me water, a napkin and wiped the counter. All of a sudden she was giving me excellent service and attention. Although I noticed the extra attention, I was in my own little world at the time. I noticed how much the oval cup resembled a breast as she refilled the coffee.

In those days I took sugar in my coffee. As I drank it, little drops of the sweetened coffee dried on the edge of the cup. I was relaxing, enjoying the feeling of not driving and just "went away" in my mind. I noticed the sweet taste of coffee around the edge of the cup and licked the sweetness with my tongue. I got a little lost in the taste of the coffee, the warmth, and the sensual shape of the cup as I licked at the the edge of the cup. Then I heard a door slamming. I did not think anything of this - Lick.

After that I heard another door slam, louder this time. *"Perhaps I should see what this is all about,"* I thought, and I opened my eyes, bringing myself back from my reverie. I was sitting at the counter with the breast-shaped cup held over my head and I was licking the bottom of the cup. All of the people in the cafe had stopped what they were doing. Stunned in shocked silence and disbelief, many held forks half way to still opened mouths. Other mouths were agape. Stares were prominent. There was no sound, no movement.

As I came to myself, I slowly lowered the cup. The waitress came through a doorway behind the counter. Her buttons were more undone and she was shaking. The noise I had heard was her slamming the door to get my attention. The door looked to lead into a hallway in back. She had been waiting in the passageway in hopes that I would follow her there. She was standing there, white in the face, shaken to the core. *Oh, God*, I thought, *how embarrassing.* I placed the cup on the counter, left a tip and paid the bill to her at the door. She was shaking. I did not know what to say to her so I just said, "Thank you" and left. I really did not wish to cause such a disturbance. Embarrassed; but laughing quietly to myself, I drove off into the night.

By the time I got back to Los Angeles I was really excited about the coming adventure. I so wanted to help build the new commune that Gar said the Rainbow Family was going to create.

First, I went to Occidental Life Insurance Company to quit my job. It was no problem for them because by then I had been away for almost two months. Free from work again, I went home and began to get my things together for a big moving sale. I had been living with my friend Kent, on Scott Avenue, since February. Later we would live together again, but that was in another life yet to unfold.

I had been so busy with the Renaissance Faire that I had not noticed the man across the street. His name was Bob, and while I had not noticed him, he had indeed been noticing me. Now I had time to get to know him. We spent my last few days in Los Angeles together, and he helped me with selling my things.

When I left he gave me a wonderful poem that he had written for and about me.

> Michael
> Beautiful birds flying against the evening sky gaze
> upon you as the morning sun shines upon you.
> Man/child the joy of life is with you.
> Teacher who gives with love.
> Student who receives with innocence.
> Father who guides with strength.
> Brother who loves with gentleness.
> Son who will accept goodness.
> Lover who is now.
>> Michael.
> Beautiful still
>> walking in worn Levi's and tennis shoes.
> Tan skin glowing in the sun.
> Rain falling softly on fawn hair.
> Eyes seeing beauty everywhere.
> Quick slow smile.
> Rough smooth hands.
> Sinewy strong body.
> A field of wildflowers that never die.
> A mountain that never grows weak.
> A river that never runs dry.
> Michael. Angel of nature,
> for you - - love.

Needless to say, this poem has become one of my prized treasures.

I headed back up to Oregon, ready to start a new life, but it was with a new-felt longing that I finally left Los Angeles. To find, then to leave so soon, someone of such a depth of feeling toward me; and I had deep feelings for him as well. Sadly, we were never to see each other again.

Several times in my life I have either sold or given away most of my belongings. I am pleased with my non-attachment attitude to possessions. Beginning in 1970 when I gave everything away and became a hippie, I have had this same disattachment ever since.

I had planned on arriving at the Rainbow Gathering on July 4th (1978). I had a week or so to explore and I wanted to see the heart of western Oregon. Since I had time to wander I took the roads that went from the ocean to the inland and back again, criss-crossing the area between the Interstate and the ocean to see the sights. Trees lined the roads so densely that I could barely see beyond them.

Mostly all I saw on these side roads were trees, and trucks loaded with trees that went speeding by. However, I was enjoying the freedom that I had, just to drive. There really isn't a lot to see in that part of Oregon except the trees which the loggers leave to line the road. Oregon exports vast amounts of trees from this part of the state, so other than the lumber trucks speeding back and forth, there was little traffic.

A slow-driving stoned hippie was not welcomed by the truck drivers. Since these roads have only two lanes, it is illegal to pass a slower vehicle. One does not travel leisurely through this part of Oregon. One either speeds up or gets run over. A giant truck grill forged into large chrome fangs, looming in my rear view mirror, made this vastly clear to me. Forcing the gas pedal to the floor I sped up, just barely keeping ahead of the truck which had no intention of slowing down for me. I was speeding down the road when I noticed an opening coming up between the trees, a turn-out place in the road ahead. It was a very small turn-out but I jerked the wheel, turned into it and slammed on the brakes as the truck sped past down the road.

Shaken and stunned, I got out of the car. It was humid to the point of being wet, yet I found the temperature was gentle and the wetness exhilarating. The trees had grown densely together in this wonderful moistness. The turn-out had been cut through thick forest growth. As I caught my breath and started to calm down again I noticed an opening between the trees, almost like a natural doorway.

I walked through the opening to find that I had entered into an area where the trees were growing in a natural circle about 40 feet across. The circle was filled with moist ferns no higher than my waist, reaching out to the sun. I had an intense feeling about the area, that I had come upon a Holy place. There was a fawn directly opposite, just standing between the trees, watching me. I walked slowly and with reverence toward the center of the circle of trees. The fawn and I watched each other as I found my way.

As I neared the center, the holy feeling of the place became more profound. It was so very peaceful there. I wanted to give something of myself. There was a song that I had been singing while I was driving that made me cry. I began to sing *Hey, That's No Way To Say Good bye* by Roberta Flack. As I sang I began to cry and I leaned over to let my tears fall among the ferns. Then energy came up from the ground through my feet, passed through my body and out through my hands which were stretched down toward the earth. Time passed and I felt cleansed and purified. The fawn was gone and it was time to go.

I could not see the opening through which I had entered but I did see another open space between the trees. I entered and found myself in yet another area tightly circled by trees. This area was much the same size but oval shaped. It was a much more beautiful place, yet this area did not have the same feeling of holiness.

There were fern-like trees raising 15 to 20 feet in height with branches stretching outward 8 to 12 feet, spread-fingered at the ends three foot wide, as thin as two inches. They were growing effortlessly straight out from the trunks, gently floating up and down on wisps of air, the fronds tenderly dripping rain drops from the fingered ends to the ferns below. The natural beauty of this place was overwhelming to me, yet walking through it helped me to come back to myself.

Soon I was back on the road and after that I did pay attention to the logging trucks that sped after me. I followed the map that I had been given. The directions were easy. They led me to Eugene, Oregon. From the place where I parked the car to the gathering was a long hike up into the mountains. I was really excited as I carried my camping gear into the forest. When I got there I found a great valley filled with a group of differing peoples. It was fascinating to see. I was told that there were 10,000 people there and I believed it!

I found a place to pitch my tent; it seemed the thing to do. Someone said that two days before, a girl had fallen from the cliffs and was killed. When the girl was found, all the people gathered in the center of the valley and meditated or chanted together and individually, sending her strength. It had been raining for months straight in Oregon. As the people gathered together, three rainbows appeared in the skies and it stopped raining. It remained clear and warm for the rest of the gathering. The day that she died, July fourth, was the same day that I had the encounter with the fawn in the clearing.

In this mountainous area I felt the power of people joining together with a common cause. Walking around I saw Hari-Krishna's cooking great pots of rice and Gypsies and "road people." I saw each person involved in being where they were and doing what they were doing, or so it seemed to me. . . I promptly had an overwhelming desire for a cup of coffee. There was none to be found, so I hiked the ten miles back out to my car, went into town, and bought a cup of coffee. Of course, I stayed in town that night and had breakfast (with coffee) in the morning before I left.

It was not lost on me, as I returned to the Rainbow Gathering, that I had hiked around 20 miles and stayed in town just for a cup of coffee.

I really didn't know what to do once I got back to the gathering, so I looked for a place where I could meditate. I found one in the clearing where the people gathered. There were many people there, enjoying the sun as it showed through clear skies. I took off all of my clothes and sat, meditating in this field. Then I ate: The Krishnas were feeding people, bless their hearts!

In the early evening there was to be a "Medicine Circle." Of course I went. People were sitting in a huge circle around one man. He was so natural in his skin that I do not remember if he even wore clothes. He told us that the purpose of sitting in a circle was to show each of us that no matter where you sat in the circle, no one would see the same thing in the same way. This is why it was called a Medicine Circle. The American

Indians always sat in a Medicine Circle when they gathered.

He also said that when the time came for a person to meet their fate, each would be at the appointed time and place, even if it took the breaking of a bone to do it. This statement, of course, carried a great deal of personal meaning for me. I went to sleep in my tent that night. The following morning, after tea and cereal, I met a young gay guy named Shandelle. Shandelle told me that he was a witch and that he lived in San Francisco. I have to say, after all the things that I had been through, I didn't think I was a slouch with that witching stuff either, so we hit it off immediately.

We went to look at the billboards where people posted notes about things: meetings, thoughts or "looking for" notes. Someone had written a note saying, "Where are all of my gay brothers and sisters?" Over it, in very bold writing, someone had written "Queers, get out of Oregon!" Shocked, Shandelle and I looked at each other. It did not take us long to make up our minds to leave the gathering. Shandelle had been hitchhiking and I was driving, so we teamed up and hiked the ten miles back out to my car.

The Rainbow Gathering behind us, we were heading for San Francisco when we came upon the giant redwoods of Humboldt County.

Chapter 10

The Mountain

The redwood groves begin very abruptly. One is in the open and then immediately surrounded with old growth forest. The feeling is impressive, to say the least. The trees have a magic unto themselves and we were ready for it. A witch and I, all charged up and looking for adventure. The trees themselves, seemed to call to us as we entered the old growth redwood forest.

It was a day of magic. The steering wheel jerked hard to the right. Upon entering the forest of the giant redwoods, Shandelle and I found ourselves in a different and enchanted world.

We left the Rainbow Gathering, which numbered about 10,000 people, because we felt that we didn't fit. A gathering of love and loving people, yet we didn't fit because we were gay. Neither Shandelle or myself felt that we were different from any of the other varied groups there. Unfortunately, others had felt differently, so we left. Are gays to be the last minority then? Perhaps.

Shandelle and I were filled with newly charged energy to join with the ancient energy of the giant redwoods. It wasn't as if I had a choice in the matter. The steering wheel had just turned to the right and I allowed it to happen. I pulled off the road and parked the car. Shandelle and I got out. Both of us were on a path of discovery but neither of us was aware of it. I looked up the road through the forest and immediately had a sense that I knew Shandelle should go in "that" direction. I pointed to the place that I felt for him and he left. I was being intensely drawn in a different direction.

The beautiful Redwood Forest

"Crack." There was that sound again. I had been hearing it in the back of my mind without really listening. "Crack." within the forest the reverberation was calling to me. I began to run toward the sharp repeating sound. There was a giant redwood tree that had fallen centuries earlier, laying in stages of partial decay beside the road and gradually turning into the ground which had sustained it and from which it came, ancient even beyond the 2,000 year old living trees that surrounded it.

"Hurry," a voice said, "he's been going on like that for days."

The voice came from the decaying tree. Strangely, the only thought that came into my head was, *"I wonder how many decades a tree this old would call days.*

The trees in the forest had a distinct sense of "being" about them, with a consciousness, a knowingness, and a growing feeling. They also fall over on occasion, and have been known to trap an unsuspecting person beneath them as they fell, causing leaning trees to be called "widow makers" by the locals. The cracking sound was coming from deep within the forest. The sound had a rhythmic quality to it, sounding deep and ominous.

As I entered the forest there was a steep drop from the road to the forest floor. The road divided a mountain into a hill growing up on one side and descending steeply down the other. Climbing carefully down the hill, I followed the cracking sound. The forest itself is a vast system of huge and ancient trees, some growing and strong, some fallen over each other in crisscross patterns, weaving themselves into a maze across the forest floor.

These giant trees, even when fallen over, are huge. It was difficult at best to go any distance at all within the forest. Trees which had fallen over often blocked my pathway. To walk around one of these giants was a task indeed. I had to walk long distances just to get to the other side. Others, a mere 12 feet high (on their sides) I could climb over. The redwoods, for the most part don't so much die but "transform." They fall over, generally from their own weight, then they decay back into the earth from which they grow again. Ferns and even other redwoods grow from the roots.

The root systems, ripped from the earth as giant trees give way, present themselves as massive fans, spread out and reaching up to four or five stories high. They also leave huge holes as wide as the roots, lined with assorted tangled ferns, parts of other trees and the remaining roots. These holes were impossible for me to cross.

To follow the sound into the forest I had to make my way around these holes and climb around the twisted maze of fallen giants as best I could. I could feel the ancient, self sustaining power in these trees and the way they had of decaying to become the very soil from which they thrived. Sustaining themselves with themselves. It was an introduction to me, an introduction to the trees and to a new way of thinking.

Deeper and deeper I followed the cracking sound into the forest. I followed the sound until high above me I could see limbs from two different trees that were rubbing against one another. One tree was leaning toward the other, and one of its limbs was pushing heavily down onto a limb of the other tree. As the wind blew, it pushed against the limb creating pressure until the heavy, upper branch released with a cracking sound.

I wanted to see why the tree was leaning so I walked toward it. The trees produce thick bark in lines that define its development as it grows. I could see that this tree had twisted as it grew; almost as if it had twirled itself into evolution. Using the lines of bark as guides from the top, I walked around the massive tree following the lines from the top where the trees were touching, down its length, I found myself in front of an opening in the tree itself. It is a testament to the size of the tree that I had to follow the lines of bark from the top to lead me.

Lightning had struck it at some point in time and there had been a fire that had burned a large hole into the trunk which caused the weakness and the leaning of the tree. I was able to walk into the hole without stooping and I could stretch out my arms without touching the sides. I wanted to help the tree.

I remembered using light as energy in Griffith Park sometime earlier, in another world it seemed, though only a few short weeks had passed. I brushed the top of my head as I had done in the park and allowed light to come in. Then I stretched out my arms and released energy into the tree, pushing up, upward into the heart of the tree. Then I heard a "thump thump" response from deep within and high above. "Thump, thump." The limbs above were sliding back and forth against each other, reverberating down through the depths of the giant tree, like a giant heart beating.

I made my way back to the car feeling somehow changed by the experience. When I met Shandelle back at the car, he told me that he had also had a deep spiritual experience, totally different but equally as meaningful to him as mine was to me.

We drove on. After a short while the steering wheel again pulled sharply to the right. I parked the car and as we got out I again sensed a direction for him to go. "Go down the road about 50 feet and you will find a way into the forest off to the right," I told him. I could see the opening in my mind. I went off to the left again, down to the forest floor.

I was just wandering within the forest when I came upon a group of mammoth trees growing in a circle. Most of the forest grows in a very random fashion which is made precarious by fallen trees. Here were giants living in an orderly "community" with each other. I also noted that there were no fallen trees within the circle. Two thousand years and more these trees had grown in this circle, and I knew that they felt and knew of each other. I wanted to be at the exact center of these ancient trees.

I found the center of the trees by watching high above where the tree tops reached out to each other, guiding me to the center of the circle. As I stood in the center of this grouping of trees; I realized that they could also sense each other through their intertwined roots. I could feel an intimacy among these trees. I knew that I could not stand there long enough for the trees to sense that I was there and I began to cry with a longing for these beings in tree form to feel my presence. As I was crying, a redwood frond (like a leaf) fell upon my head. I thought; *This must be what a tiny cone must undergo as it falls from the tree and waits to germinate and grow.* Being gently covered with fronds to protect it from the winter to come, one frond at a time. Then I felt that I was one with the trees, and I cried tears of happiness.

On my way back to the car, I saw at my feet a peculiar short piece of tree. Moss had grown around it. I picked it up to find a decayed center of a tree, the very top of a tree which had grown over a thousand years and had fallen over to decay for four centuries more. Less than a foot long, it had the perfect core of a tree, with little nubs that showed where limbs had grown outward. I took it home with me and called it, The Heart of the Redwoods.

When I got back to the car, I found that Shandelle was not there so I went to the opening that I had pointed out to him and went in. It was a mass of covered growth, thin branches intertwined in webs. Moss and ferns grew in abundance but I saw no pathway. I pushed my way past some branches, and promptly fell about 12 feet onto the rocks of a dry riverbed. *I will not break any bones!* I affirmed to myself as I fell, and no bones were broken but it sure did hurt. Among the rocks were gentle mosses that had grown in beautiful forms. Now many were crushed by my intrusion.

Trying not to disturb anything else in the riverbed, I painfully climbed back up to the top and limped my way out to the road. As I was making my way back to the car I saw a sort of opening and gently stepped within. I went only a little ways when I saw a large bird, as big as a human, and I knew it was Shandelle. Quietly, I continued back to the car to leave him alone.

After telling my story, I asked Shandelle about the opening I had pointed out. "I couldn't find any way in," I told him. Shandelle gave me a quizzical look and told me that he hadn't had any problem getting in at all. It has been a lesson for me ever since: "One cannot walk another person's pathway."

Our day was spent with several of these adventures. Each time the steering wheel announced when to stop, heralding a new spiritual event about to unfold. I could always feel the great forest reaching out to me in one direction and I could also feel it calling for Shandelle.

Both of us had experienced incredible, powerful, and magical things. This time was to be different. The steering wheel had jerked to the left, toward a dirt fire road used by the forest service to get equipment into the woods. My feeling this time was that Shandelle was to join me. Together we were going to share an encounter. I parked the car and got out. "It's up here," I said.

I was drawn toward the road that wandered up a hill to the left. Excitedly, I rushed to the road and began to climb. As I was climbing I became aware of an energy coming from the bottom of the hill behind me. I turned toward the energy. As I did, my hands were drawn out as if by a magnet, stretching toward the bottom of the hill. I stood there, arms outstretched, astonished as I felt the connection with the force.

There was a sound of endless talking as Shandelle, vocal as always, made his way up the road. "What does it look like I'm doing?" I asked angrily. "Looks like you're conjuring something," came the reply. "I am, and this is a very powerful place, so either shut up or go back to the car," I darted back. Then I turned my back on the astonished witch and stomped up the road.

I walked a few paces then turned to see if Shandelle was following me. He had turned around and was heading back down the hill. I was furious and started down toward him. Then a force like a giant hand grabbed the top of my head and twisted me around with such a power that my left foot flew off of the ground and I was left facing the top of the hill.

I was stunned. I had seen and felt many things that day, but the dynamic force such as this was a totally different phenomenon.

I became aware of three things then: One, that this was to be a powerful spiritual encounter for me alone. Two, that I was very angry and I knew that was no way to enter into a spiritual event. And three, that I had been trying to control Shandelle.

I spent a few moments calming myself. I also felt a bit sheepish about trying to control Shandelle. I forced myself to appreciate that Shandelle had to leave in order for me to be alone. Slowly, I got rid of the anger and filled myself with the love that I had been feeling all day. Then I began again to climb the hill. After taking a few steps, I remembered the force that I had felt at the base of the hill. I turned to where I had felt the power and reached out my hands. The power again grabbed my hands and pulled with an extreme and compelling attraction.

Time passed. I stood there, arms outstretched, waiting for something to happen and wondering what was to come. I really wanted to go to the top of the mountain, not stand there facing downward; yet the power was at the base, not at the top. Then, I again remembered the power I was able to contact by working with light and energy.

I brushed the top of my head and allowed light to shine inside. Then I brushed the "Third Eye" area in front of my forehead and allowed light to shine out, focusing the light so that it went through my outstretched hands toward the power at the base of the hill. Once I felt a connection with the power, I slowly began to turn to the right, my outstretched hands guiding the beam of light which was connected to the power at the base of the hill. As I turned, I could feel the power moving from the bottom of the hill, following the light beam and moving from the bottom of the hill until the power was at the top. Now I could follow the power and go to the top of the hill as well.

As I walked, I came upon a crushed beer can and picked it up to help clean the area. Not knowing what to do with it, I put it in my back pocket. I still have that can. Then I came to a small tree on my left. It was vibrating in a way that told me it was not just a tree. I stopped in front of the tree and bowed slightly in recognition of its special vibrancy. As I stood there, it seemed to grow wings and feathers and then it turned into a bird. I remember growing feathers and doing the same. We were flying counter-clockwise down into a cone-like canyon which resembled the inside of a volcano. It was just a momentary thing and I found myself again facing the tree.

I noticed that I had become quite cold (a feeling I have never enjoyed), so I bowed to the tree in thanks and ran down the hill to the car to get warm. I was also very eager to tell Shandelle of all that had happened.

There was no one at the car. I put my jacket on to get warm. I realized that I had cut the adventure short just because I was cold. Scolding myself for my "weakness," I raced back up the road to the tree. I was delighted to see that it was still vibrating.

Again, I reached out my arms to find the power at the bottom of the hill. My arms were grabbed and held out-stretched. I reached inside my head and opened again the pathway for the light, in through the top of my head and out through my third eye, to be released between my outstretched hands.

As I focused my mind upon the light and the moving of the power, I thought of a key within a lock, a very special lock with a very special key. Again I turned toward the top of the hill, pulling the power along with me. As I completed the revolution this time, everything was different. The entire hilltop was vibrating with an energy that was palpable. Somehow, I knew that I had to walk with my eyes closed. Slowly, step by step, I started walking toward the top of the hill.

I stepped upon a rock and stumbled a bit. For some reason it made me think of Jesus as he stumbled carrying the cross. I took a few more steps and felt something brush my left cheek. I realized that I was heading just a bit to the left and I thought the brushing was from leaves of a tree on the side of the road. I corrected my course a bit and continued. After a few more steps I felt something ever so slightly brush my right cheek. I felt that the leaves of the trees were guiding me again and I was going too far to the right. Then it came to me that it could not be leaves from the trees that were brushing my cheeks, the road was too wide for me to reach both sides with just the few steps that I had taken. So I peeked a bit to see just how far apart the trees really were. There were trees and brush on both sides of the road, but none were close enough to touch me. I had to accept that this adventure was not limited by everyday rules.

After a few more blind steps I felt a 'presence' and I knew that I had "arrived." I opened my eyes to find a huge mountain in front of me. It was shaped like a perspective point drawing, with vanishing points at the sides and the corner, the largest edge directly in front of me defined by sharp lines almost like facing the edge of a tall building in a large city. The perspective was such that I could not tell if the mountain was right in front of me or miles away.

There were three distinct layers to the mountain: The lowest was smooth, as if made of a slate-like material with a feeling of an opening on the lower left side. The next layer was broken up in huge pieces that resembled great teeth. The last, the top, was growing with bushes and brush.

From the bushes there arose three poles, like flag poles or limbless trees. There was another pole that had fallen down or perhaps had never been erected. I thought I was to climb the mountain and erect the one pole that was laying down. I admit that I was delighted to find that was not the case. I remembered thinking of Jesus moments before, and I said to the mountain, "I thirst," and I really did.

Then from the mountain I could see a small bubble coming towards me. The bubble was white pearlescent and writhing with livingness, like watching oil on the top of water. The bubble grew as it approached, increasing to about the size of a basketball. As it came closer, I encircled it with my arms in an embrace. It burst into millions of "pieces," like water droplets, going all over my body. It was as if each droplet were sponging the pores of my skin. The individual pieces seemed to join then into one amoeba like form.

The feeling was so energizing and ecstatic that I was barely able to continue standing.

"Do you accept this as your lover?" I heard the mountain asking. ("This" was not the actual word that was used, but the feeling was clear to me). "Yes, oh yes," I replied. I was about to faint with exhilaration when from my left there stepped a naked American Indian. I knew that this Indian was me (or a part of me, as a part of my heritage is Indian). The Indian said "Wait a minute," or words to that effect. "You are so gullible." (The word was not "you, I or we," whatever it was, it meant "we both".) "We don't know anything about this creature, we don't know what it is, we don't even know its name." The Mountain then quietly said, "The name is Love."

I stood there hoping my "Indian side" hadn't ruined things for me. I was left facing the mountain and "Love" was gone. I wanted to give something to the Mountain so I brushed the top of my head to let light in and I brushed the front of my head to let light out. I pushed and pushed but there was no light as there had been at earlier times. Then I thought of sparklers that we used to play with when I was a child. I envisioned the sparklers inside of my head and light began to shine.

A voice came to me then, a voice that I have heard before both in dreams and in waking moments. A woman's voice saying gently, "You would do better if you lost your identity."

I saw an image of myself with light shining from the top and the front of my head. As I watched the vision, a portion of my head seemed to break away and light shone out from the missing part. Slowly and gently I caused parts of myself (in the vision) to fall away. Soon the vision was gone. It was my real body that was going away. My body parts were dropping away and being replaced with light as I let my body go. I admit that I had a bit of difficulty with the sex parts, they kept coming back. I remember saying, "Not now," as I gently made the feelings go away.

At the point where there was none of "me" left, there appeared a golden flame. The flame did not burn, but was alive and moving slowly in a flame-like manner.

It then grew downward forming a golden spike which "disappeared" into a clear jelly like extension, reappearing as a silver spike which came to a point and disappeared.

In the jelly like stuff, there were small symbols. The stuff was transparent and was difficult to see. I believe I felt as much as I saw them. The entire flame symbol seemed to be alive and was floating in the most beautiful blue sky with the whitest puffy clouds I could imagine. The amoeba like figure of "Love" was flying all about and through this wonderful vision.

I had been given my own symbol in a series of dreams during the previous months. I caused my symbol to be raised in the center of the clear stuff, and it was accepted. As it was accepted into the clear stuff I realized that it was part of my larger symbol.

Then it was over. The vibrations ceased, the symbols disappeared, (although as I think back, I believe The Mountain was still there). I had to pee, so I relieved myself upon a rock. *Very natural*, I thought, and I ran back down to the car to find Shandelle. "Get out your pad and pencil," I said - - - "Have I got a story to tell you."

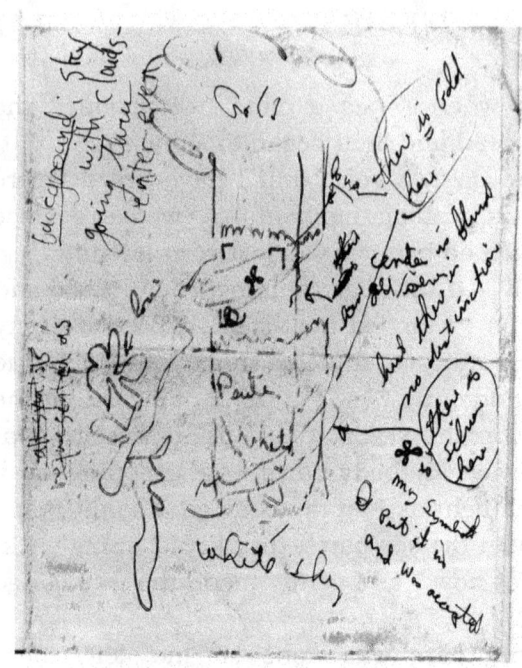

The Flame symbol.
Quickly drawn
as soon as I
got back to the car.

Later I made a drawing with less detail
but also including The Mountain.

Faces peer out from trees
and fairy tale scenes
appear, in the
magical Redwood Forest.

Normal waking consciousness is not innocent of all the other traces of existence, or devoid of other kinds of awareness. It is only because you usually use your waking consciousness in limited ways that you do not encounter these clues with any regularity. They are always present. Following them can give you some idea of those other directions, and levels.

Often seemingly unrelated symbols or images may rise into your mind. Usually you ignore them. If instead you acknowledge them and turn your attention to them, you can follow them to several other layers with ease.

A single image may suddenly open up into an entire mental landscape, but you will know none of this if you do not acknowledge the first clues that are just beneath present awareness, if you are only willing to look.

   Seth Speaks, by Jane Roberts

Chapter 11

After the Mountain

I had planned to build a life with the people at the Rainbow Gathering, so again I had no home and no idea what to do next. The Mountain experience had moved me profoundly. Nevertheless; the Northern California Renaissance Faire was coming up. I wanted to act in it again, so I moved in with a friend named Bobby, who lived in Oakland, not too far from the faire site.

Traveling was easy for me at the time. I had quit my job and was looking for a new way of life. I wanted to change again. A month earlier I had gone to the Rainbow Gathering looking for a home but I found incredible spiritual experiences in the Redwoods instead. I was now staying with my friend Bob, in Oakland, waiting for faire rehearsals to begin.

I found a Ford F-100, just what I wanted, in Crescent City, about 300 miles away just north of the Humboldt Redwoods. I took a bus to Crescent City to see the truck. It was love at first sight, so I bought it and drove it back. Since the route back went straight through the redwoods, driving back through the forest and staying the night was never in question.

As I entered the forest I parked next to the old decaying tree stump that had talked to me on my previous trip. The tree did not speak this time, but then, I didn't expect it to. I performed a pranam to it in respect as I passed by. It was deep into the forest to which I wanted to return. I remembered the great holes left by the giant roots torn from the ground as trees fell over. I recognized fallen trees that I had worked my way across, over and through on my last visit to the forest, so it was easier for me to find my way this time.

Before long I was able to find the tree that had been leaning precariously into its neighbor. If it hadn't found another tree to lean against it certainly would have become a widow maker. The limb that had been pushing down and rubbing against the other tree was now about three feet away from the other tree. Free from the rubbing of the neighboring limb, there was no longer a cracking sound reverberating within the forest. It seems the energy that I had sent to the tree had made a difference and the forest was in silence and at peace. Passing the great stump, I remembered the words that it had spoken before; "Hurry, he's been going on like this for days." I was smiling with joy as I got back into my truck.

As I drove down the road toward the campground, I saw a great tree that had fallen parallel to the road. I couldn't help but notice the length of this giant as I passed. The root system was extraordinarily huge. It seemed to me that it had been an unusually tall tree. I had an intense desire to explore this colossal tree, so I parked my truck and walked back toward the roots. There was a giant hole where the roots had been ripped from the ground with the falling of the tree. The roots themselves fanned out six or seven stories far above me. This was by far the largest root system that I had yet encountered. I had a longing to climb upon the tree and be in that root system; the place from which the tree had sustained its life, now a place of its death.

The tree was so huge it would have been impossible for me to climb onto it from the root end so I had to walk the length of the tree toward the top where it would be narrow enough for me to climb.

Walking beneath the huge; barreled outside of the tree, the gigantic trunk loomed far above me, up and outward like a curving shelter as the tree stretched out from the roots. I walked alongside the massive fallen redwood, touching it as I went. I was dwarfed under the side of the tree that was curving out above me. It took a while, but finally I made my way near what used to be the top. The girth was only about 12 feet thick and I felt that I would be able to climb onto the tree at this point. The bark was very thick and easy to use as hand and footholds.

Standing upon the tree I could see the enormous fan of roots reaching out and up into the sky above me. When I looked behind me I could see the tree stretching out, growing into nothingness as the "top" dissolved back into dirt.

I walked reverently toward the roots. As I walked the length of the tree, its great vastness made me realize that indeed it had been a living thing, several thousand years old, and now it was dead. The gigantic root system grew larger as I approached, until it splayed upward in multi-storied heights above me. As I got closer, the feelings within me turned to grief for this great giant, and I threw myself within the root system and cried with deep grief for this being.

"Don't be sad," a voice said. "You will understand as you leave." I finally quit crying and rose to go. Where I had been lying, I saw an earring, just like an old-time pirate would wear. *Just what I need for my part in the Renaissance Faire*, I thought. What a great gift! With my new treasure in hand, I decided to walk the entire length of the tree. I wanted to go from these enormous roots to the other end, the top of which was disappearing in perspective in front of me.

As I walked away from the roots which were very thick and massive, the tree grew less broad. At one point there was a branch of another tree that crossed in front of me and I had to move it out of my way. As I moved the branch aside I could not help but notice the difference in this year's new growth compared to the growth of previous seasons, for the new growth was a much lighter green.

Gently, I took a frond, put the new growth into my mouth, and bit it off. When I had swallowed it, I pushed my own spit into the remaining needle as an exchange of energy from one to another, and I continued to walk down to the "top" of the tree. The tree was so long that when I came to where it was only a foot or so in width I became impatient and was tempted to jump down and go on my way. I'm glad to say that I kept on walking.

The tree grew smaller and smaller as I approached the top, until near the end it became a rounded mound of decaying matter;a small elongated pile of tree becoming earth.

I stood from that end and turned around. Looking back, I saw the mound of earth become the slender top of the tree which then grew as it went away from me to become the giant fan of roots. I saw that from these roots, another very large tree was growing. The new tree was so large that I had not even seen it, yet I had been there with it at the trunk. It was from this re-birthed tree that I had sucked and given back my own energy.

The tree was not dying, it was just "turning over" and being born anew. *You will understand as you leave*, swept into my consciousness. Thus it was that I learned a secret of life and death within the giant redwood forest.

In the morning, I looked for places that I had visited on my prior visit. I found the fire road that I had taken to see The Mountain, but it was not the same. Somehow I did not really expect it to be so; I knew that I was not meant to travel the same road twice. Happily, I drove my "new" truck back to Oakland to act again in the faire.

I played several characters that season: Michael the valet and poor Styx the would-be thief.. Also during that season I got picked to play a part on stage. The director who was casting for the part asked me if I could do a stage fall. I had never done one before. Truth be known, I didn't really know what a stage fall was. I just allowed myself to fall straight backwards onto the stage, praying that I wouldn't break anything.

I did not break anything. It didn't even hurt. The director was impressed and I got the part. Thus I became the "Harvest Hag" in the Noon show, the largest show in the Faire. One day a fellow actor asked me if I was the one playing the Harvest Hag. He said there was a man trying to find out who the actor was. A few days later I found an article pinned on a bulletin board back stage. It was from the Wall Street Journal and the headline read: "From Twilzywhop to Hag, all the world's a stage." I knew that I was the only Hag at the faire so I took the article. It was describing the Faire. In one paragraph they had written: "Nearby the hag of the harvest shrieks, And all I touch shall wither."

I remember an ad on TV around that time. People were talking about money and someone quoted his stock broker, "My broker at XXX said,- - - " everybody stopped talking to listen to his stock broker's quote. It seems that the Wall Street Journal, probably the most prestigious of financial papers, had quoted me.

Each faire I made it a point to buy one thing that I wanted; there were things available at the faire that one could not get anywhere else. At this faire, I found a wonderful watermelon tourmaline crystal mounted in silver with a silver chain. I was just walking around with the crystal around my neck when a woman came up to me, took hold of the crystal, and said, "Ah! You have a magic crystal."

Later that day I needed to go from one end of the faire to another in a hurry. The faire site was large with several thousand actors and visitors; people who expected my character to interact with them but I didn't have the time. I remembered the lady's words about the crystal being magic. So I held it between my fingers and said to myself, "I'm invisible." I walked through the Fairgrounds, in the center of the road, holding the crystal and the thought.

Everyone, it seemed, looked away from me. People who passed by me looked toward the ground or somewhere other than at me. I was indeed invisible to them simply because they did not look at me. I stood in front of the Russian Piroshki booth waiting for Constantine to notice me. It was Constantine who I had come to meet. He looked at me for several minutes without really seeing me. Then he shook his head with a start because he finally saw me standing there in front of him. I was to go to Mendocino with Constantine that week between the Faire times, which were only held on the weekends.

Playing the Harvest hag on stage wasn't really a demanding role, but projecting my voice to the back rows from an outdoor stage was difficult, and a good lesson for me to learn.

When the faire came to an end I went up to spend some time with Constantine in Mendocino. Mendocino is a sleepy little town next to the ocean. It has its full measure of what is called, "The Albion Nation." Albion, which is a small town south of Mendocino, was named by its founder for his homeland in England. "Nations" were what the local tribes called themselves. The Albion Nation consisted of the town drunks and layabouts. They could be seen every day hanging out about both towns and certainly added color for a visitor.

While walking in the forest near Constantine's cabin, I came upon a giant mushroom. I took it back to Constantine who pronounced it a Chanterelle; one of the most favored and valuable of mushrooms. I took a big shopping bag and went back out into the forest and filled the bag full of these mushrooms. He made a wonderful soup of them that night. Chanterelles are really very delicious.

I also met Constantine's best friend whose name was Don. Don did odd jobs around the area. During the Christmas season he also made wreaths from the pine branches which grew in profusion there. Don invited me to stay with him in November, just before Christmas and help him make wreaths. I accepted.

I was at a loss for what to do until November, the time when Don said we could start, so I decided to go to Salt Lake City and see my relatives. It seems that I always went to Salt Lake to see relatives when I had the time.

I was driving through Nevada when I came upon a town named Fallon. I remembered having a great-aunt named Ruby who lived in Fallon. I hadn't seen her since I was a little boy. It was morning and I wanted to eat. I found a phone book and looked to see if my great-aunt was listed. Ruby Rose was indeed listed and I called. "Do you want to have breakfast with your great nephew?" I asked. "Hell yes!" she replied. Thus; I again met my great-aunt Ruby.

We had breakfast at a small restaurant and talked a bit, then I said I had to move on. I didn't really need to go. No one expected me. Again, I seemed to be the only one who felt the need to "be somewhere." I had not yet learned to accept life as it presented itself and was still living out plans that I had made, so I continued on my way.

About five miles out of town, something in the U-joint broke. Although I didn't know much about car repair, Jay had taught me that when there was trouble with a vehicle it had to be either an electrical, mechanical, or a fuel problem. Once that was isolated, the problem could be approached with greater ease. One look under the truck however, and I could tell right away that this was a job for a clothes hanger. Happily I always kept one in back of the seat for just such occasions. I was able to tie the driveshaft into position and limp back to Fallon.

Styx, wearing the magic crystal and getting ready to perform in Hamlet.

There were only four actors playing all of the parts which added greatly to the comedy.

Leaving the truck at the local mechanic, I went back to spend the night with a delighted Aunt Ruby. We had a great night together. She fixed us beans for dinner; she made great beans.

Aunt Ruby and her husband Harry never had much money. When they got married during the depression they hitched rides on freight trains to go on their honeymoon. This was my Aunt Ruby. She had no pretensions. She was just Ruby. "And to hell with anyone who doesn't like it!"

She had a hunched back and wasn't the prettiest person around unless you looked at her heart or her honest and straight forwardness. I had told her a story about my life with my family. "Hell, if my family treated me like that," she said, "I'd never go back to see them."

In the morning my truck was fixed and I was on my way. Not far outside of town the road split. There was a sign: An arrow pointed left toward Salt Lake City, another arrow pointed right toward The Grand Canyon. "I've never seen the Grand Canyon," I thought to myself. With only a few seconds hesitation I took the turn to the right.

About 50 feet past the turnoff there was a hitchhiker. I picked him up. His name was Rick, from Louisiana. He was just wandering, the same as me, so we decided to tour the canyon areas together. It was a beautiful day. The sky was deep blue with big puffy white clouds. By then I was hooked on photography and wanted to get some pictures, so I left the highway at the nearest road and pulled off into a field, right into a mud hole. I didn't think much about the mud hole, just about getting pictures of the beautiful sky. I even got Rick to pose naked for me.

After taking several pictures as well as enjoying a break from driving, we got back in the truck and was returning to the highway when I got stuck. Wheels spinning us deeper and deeper into the mud. Rick watched me for awhile then he asked me to let him try. I was happy to let him. Back and forth he went. He put the truck into forward then reverse, and back again; each time going just and inch or two farther until at one point the truck just kept moving forward. I was vey impressed and told him so. "Hell," he said, "I used to get stuck trucks out of the Bayou, boy."

We went camping through Zion and Bryce canyons, then the North Rim of the Grand Canyon. The canyon itself is immense, so deep and wide that entire weather systems take place inside it. At one place, called Point Royal, the canyon makes almost a 180 degree turn-about leaving a point sticking out that is almost totally encircled by the canyon as it doubles itself in vastness. At this point the canyon, which is awesome to begin with, becomes breathtaking in its magnificence.

I wanted to get as close as possible to the cliff edge itself, to where the encircling canyon seemed to be pointing, creating a "meeting point" of energy. This was in the fall. The park was officially closed for the winter, so since there was no one there to stop me I slipped past the fence.

After I climbed over the fence, the ground descended sharply, and as I neared the edge of the canyon face it became a cliff. It was so steep that I got down on my hands and knees to not slip over the side and into the canyon. As I got close to the edge of the cliff, I saw that there was a flat rock positioned at the exact center of the circling canyon. *A power spot if ever I saw one*, I thought. Slowly, I crawled to the rock. I wanted to sit on that rock but I was frightened at the same time. I would be sitting out over the edge of a sheer drop to the canyon floor. Crawling on my hands and knees, I inched closer.

All of a sudden, I became aware of a presence upon the rock. I admit I was relieved to find someone else there. Silently, I brought my knees to the edge of the rock, sat back, and began to meditate. There appeared to me a naked figure. He was a man of indistinguishable age. His body had neither hair nor wrinkles. He showed me with his expression that he was astonished that I knew he was there. I pranamed to him in acknowledgement and sat back to meditate.

"Michael, hey Michael, where are you?" Rick was trying to

find me. Not wanting the meditating monk (I assume) to be disturbed, I backed away and rejoined Rick. Rick and I enjoyed exploring together, but soon it was time to go our separate ways.

Fall was fast approaching and I went back up to Mendocino to help Don make the Christmas wreaths that we would be selling in San Francisco. In the mornings we would go collecting pine boughs. Don would weld frames from thick wire and I would wrap groups of the boughs with wire, attaching them to the frames. After the day's batch of wreaths was finished we would drive into San Francisco, and having sold the wreaths, have a good dinner and drive back up to Albion. It was fun and certainly kept me busy.

Soon I was back in Oakland with Bobby, and we celebrated Christmas together. I did some handyman work for a time but I still needed a job.

THE WALL STREET JOURNAL.

MONDAY, SEPTEMBER 18, 1978

From Beggar to Hag To Twelzie Wop, All the Faire's a Stage

Peasants Babble, Hawkers Cry At California Re-Creation Of an Elizabethan Festival

Nearby, the "hag of the harvest," a scarecrow figure with a carrot for a nose, shrieks, "All I touch shall wither!" Coming to the villagers' defense, Hermes, in a Roman toga, bounds onto the stage and engages the hag in combat. To lusty cheers, he snaps her carrot nose off.

Chapter 12

Leave California in a Puff of Smoke

It had been a decade filled with magic for me. The trips that I had taken on LSD had helped me to look beyond the three dimensions at other lives and other events that take place everyday and everywhere. I had learned so much from these journeys beyond the normal dimensions.

Settling down meant having an income. In my twenties I had worked as a bartender, and enjoyed it a lot, so I got a job at a bar in Oakland named "Grandma's House."

"Woof." There was a distinct bark. "Woof." There it was again, it was coming from the kitchen. I staggered out of bed and made my way to the kitchen. It had been a long night at the bar. There in the middle of the kitchen floor sat a black puppy, wagging her tail at me. "Who are you?" I asked. She didn't answer; she just sat there and wagged her tail. "Well, don't bark any more," I said, and I went back to bed.

"Woof," she barked again. I was at home alone and really wanted some more sleep. "OK, you can lie down next to my bed," I told her. I climbed back into bed assured that I could sleep this time. A cold nose was soon pressed upon my back. "All right, you can sleep with me just this once," I told her, "But never again." Immediately she jumped into bed with me. I put my arm around her and we both went to sleep.

Thus, I acquired Lady, a Black Lab and Golden Retriever mix; a wonderful blend of loyalty, love and gentleness. My friend, Bobby, had found her in a warehouse where he worked. Someone had abandoned her there. I had had a dog for most of my life. As a small boy and throughout most of my adult life I was seldom without one.

Jon and I even had a pair of miniature apricot poodles while we lived together in Silverlake before I became a hippie. "Shrka and Misty" were apricot poodles. They had a litter of pups that were used in a Gaines dog food commercial. Now a dog was coming into my life once again. With Lady, I found that a female Lab/Golden Retriever mix was the perfect dog for me.

Lady was the first of three dogs that I had of this combination. Each one had the same calm and loyal disposition and each was to complement my life beautifully. Lady was followed by Maggie, then Sandy who was a companion for Maggie when she got older.

Grandma's House was an easy going neighborhood bar and sometimes I was able to take Lady to work with me. She was a very friendly dog and loved the attention the patrons showered on her. I had been working there for several months when Lady came along. I enjoyed working at the bar and the locals who frequented there as well. Maybe I could have stayed and built a life for myself in Oakland, but fate had other plans.

I now found myself at a time of difficult growth. Quitting smoking was undoubtedly the most difficult thing I have ever had to do.

I had tried to quit several times in the past. Trying to quit is extremely difficult because "trying" means that there is another cigarette waiting sometime in the future; so instead of being finished with the habit there is a longing for that next smoke. Quitting is much easier because there is no longer another cigarette to wait for.

I had tried to quit smoking in the spring of 1978 and I actually did fine for about two weeks. One day I was helping my friend, John Coffey, give my truck a tune-up. He sprayed the motor with engine cleaner and said, "Now we just wait until it works. I usually have a cigarette while I wait," he said. "But you don't smoke so you can chew gum or something." I figured that after two weeks I could easily have only one cigarette so I smoked one, but I didn't like it. However, the following day I wanted another and I had one. Then, of course, I started smoking again.

A few weeks later, on May 1st I again tried to quit. I walked deep into Griffith Park, smoking all the way. I had decided that I would go to a point deep in the park named Bee Rock. Bee Rock formed a cliff that towered over the park below. I would throw the remaining cigarettes off the edge and would have to walk all of the way out of the park without a cigarette. Walking out of the park would give me about two hours of not smoking. I made a promise to myself that if I had another cigarette, I would buy a carton and would not try to quit again for a year. This made the next cigarette very "costly" for me. If I really wanted another cigarette I would have to go to a store and get a pack. I felt that if I could last for two hours, perhaps I could last for three, or maybe even into the evening, or possibly even really quit smoking for good. The prospect of buying a carton and not trying to quit for a year seemed to work.

But three months later, fate stepped in. I found myself sharing a room in Oakland with my friend Chris, a smoker. We were staying in Bobby's house while Chris and I acted at the Renaissance Faire in Novato. Every morning he would wake up and light a cigarette. The smell of the cigarette smoke made me ill. Each morning I endured the sick feeling, until I finally decided that to keep from getting sick, I would take up smoking again. I decided that I could quit again as soon as the Faire was over and we were no longer sleeping in the same room. This I proceeded to do.

The end of the Faire came and I did indeed begin to throw my cigarettes away. Then I remembered my promise: *If I have another cigarette, I will buy a carton and not try to quit again for a year.* I really did not want to wait for another year to quit, so I allowed myself to make May first, the day I originally made the promise, the date that I would quit once more. This still left me with nine more months to smoke, however.

The problem with working at Grandma's House was that almost everyone smoked. One customer might come in, have one cigarette and leave, but before long another would come in and do the same thing. Being almost constantly surrounded by cigarette smoke, I smoked more and more and during the coming nine months, my addiction grew so strong that soon I was smoking four packs a day.

My throat began to burn and my voice became little more than a rasped sound that somehow shaped itself around the words I was trying to say. I even had to ask customers to call "Last call" for me because I could barely speak above a whisper. I began to believe that I was developing throat cancer so I went to a doctor. "Do I have throat cancer?" I croaked. The doctor told me that I was not developing cancer at that point but that if I did not quit smoking I most certainly would develop it in the near future. "I have to wait 'till May 1st" I replied.

I told this story to a friend of mine at the bar, telling him of my promise to continue smoking until May 1st. "My health means more to me than some dumb promise," he told me. My answer was that my integrity meant more to me than my health. I hadn't really thought of it that way before, but keeping the promise I made to myself had become very important. I did continue to smoke four packs of cigarettes a day and the burning in my throat grew worse. Finally, the first of May came, the day I could finally quit smoking.

I took three days off work and went alone into the surrounding mountains with some pot and my camera. I took a puff of pot and began to shoot pictures. The lighting was absolutely beautiful and I became totally involved in the photography, creeping on the ground to get close-ups of small plants or insects. I suddenly realized that I had gone without a cigarette for two whole hours! *I stopped smoking two hours ago*, I thought, *and I didn't even notice it!*

I wondered why it had been so difficult for me to quit smoking; I had to almost allow myself to get cancer in order to quit. Sometime later, I remembered a time when I was in my teens. I was smoking a cigarette now and then, probably not addicted to them yet. I was in back of the Capitol in Salt Lake City, where I grew up. It was a very beautiful spot where one could see the lights of the city. I went there sometimes to be alone and to think. I wanted something. I can't remember what it was at that time, but I asked God for it. I promised that if I got it, I would quit smoking.

As things happen, I did get what ever it was; however, not for many weeks. *God didn't do this*, I thought, *He'd have done it faster*. Therefore, I did not quit smoking. But a promise to God is a promise to oneself. I was bound to have to face this at some time or other. Now 20 years later quitting smoking had been the hardest thing I ever had to do. I had honesty at last between me and my God. I have never wanted a cigarette since.

It had been ten years since I had given my house away, and became a hippie. Ten years and several lives later. I remembered being the programmer with all the possessions, but little depth. The visions that I had on my trips on LSD, the short time I spent with the hippies, paranormal experiences and my recent encounters in the redwoods, had changed me so much I couldn't even relate to Michael the programmer anymore. Now it was 1979 and I was growing into yet another person.

An experience that I had with my friends, Beau and Brian, gives greater meaning to the phrase "growing into yet another person." We took an acid trip together.

I went away in my mind. It was dark and moist but comfortable. Something broke and I was no longer surrounded by liquid. Then there was intense pressure and a feeling of being pulled or pushed. After a time, the pressure released but then there was a pain and something was happening to me. This was new and frightening and I made a crying sound. The first breath was not painful, but new. I did not remember any pain with the cutting of the cord.

I gulped for air as if I had been swimming up through deep water and had just splashed through the surface, struggling for breath. I could even feel the water falling away from my face as I gasped from the vision to find myself with my friends.

"I've just experienced being born!" I exclaimed.

The experience of new birth then led to a discussion about change and growth. None of us really wanted to stay in Oakland, so we cast about for a new place to move. Someone mentioned Colorado as a possible home. None of us had ever been there and it was supposed to be very beautiful.

Beau wanted to go somewhere where there was a four year college. Alamosa, Colorado has a four year college, he told us. So we decided that was where we would go. I saw on the map there were two rivers that conjoined in Alamosa. *Has to be a great place,* I thought, and we began planning for the big move.

Then I met Rodger when he came into the bar one night. He was with a date. I noticed that he was watching me, however, and as he turned to leave, I put my hand gently on his butt. He was back the next night. I was alone in the bar when he came in. Without even saying anything we promptly joined together and kissed. We had found one another and were lovers just like that.

I told Rodger that I was going to leave Oakland with Beau and Brian. We were planning on leaving within two months and I asked him to join us. He said that he could not leave with us. He had things to do before he could leave; but would join us in Colorado.

Now another Renaissance Faire was over and we were getting ready to move to beautiful Colorado.

So much had happened in such a short time: The Mountain, the magic crystal, working in Mendocino, quitting smoking at last, and meeting Rodger. Now, I was to leave California where I had lived for 20 years.

I wanted to give Bobbie and his friends a gift. There were four or five of us together at his house the night before we were to leave. I took a special glass that I had. It was shaped like a Viking drinking horn. I filled it with water and set it in the middle of the floor where we were seated in a circle. Then I took off my magic necklace and dipped the crystal into the water to where it was immersed with the mounting just touching the top of the water. Then I pulled the ends of the silver chain down to meet the floor.

Closing my eyes, I sent energy into the crystal. "What is he doing"? Someone asked. "He's blessing us," I heard Bobby tell them. Then I pulled my necklace out and put it on. I passed the glass of water to Bobbie and said, "Drink your fill and pass it on." And I closed my eyes as the glass was passed around. When it came back to me, I too, drank my fill. Then I took the necklace off and again dipped the tourmaline into the water. I pulled the edges of the chain to meet the floor. The crystal touched the water at the same place and the chain touched the table at the same place as well. There was the same amount of water in the glass as before we had drunk of it. Bobbie was right. I did bless them.

I hung the crystal from a golden chain, and I added to it the wonderful Dove of peace that the hippies had given me as I left for Europe. The combination, I found, was very powerful and I made use of its energies many times.

It had helped me to walk in invisibility and to bless and replenish the water at Bobbie's. The dove reminded me of when I had begun this journey so many years ago in Silverlake.

Years later, I bought a home in North Hollywood, California where I made an "altar place" in my closet, composed of things that I considered to be sacred. It was not a religious thing as much as a remembrance of what they represented to me. The necklace hung as the centerpiece in the center of my altar.

At that time, I rented one of my bedrooms to a gay Mormon guy named Daniel. Since I had grown up as a Mormon, I thought I could trust him but one cannot judge a book by its cover as they say. He left in the dead of night, having taken the necklace from my altar.

But that was to be years in the future. Now I was off to Colorado with Beau and Brian, and Rodger was soon to follow.

Chapter 13

Leaving Our Mark in Colorado

The preceding months had been checkered with unusual events to say the least. Lured by the reputed beauty of Colorado, I was headed toward a more normal way of life with my friends,   - - or maybe not.

I went to Colorado with Beau and Brian. We were headed for a town called Alamosa. Beau had selected it because it had a four year college and he wanted to go back to school. We had passed through a town called Durango on the way. It was a quaint little town nestled near the mountains, and downtown looked like the early 1900s. They even had a steam locomotive, The Durango & Silverton Railroad. The mountains were wonderful and the whole area seemed like a paradise.

I had seen on the map that Alamosa had two rivers coming into it. If Durango was this stunning I could only imagine how beautiful Alamosa must be. Alamosa, however, is in the middle of a desert valley, miles from the nearest mountains and barren by any standard. Beau and Brian were not daunted by the desolate town without mountains, trees or any vegetation to speak of, but I could never live happily in a place like that; especially after having seen Durango.

So I insisted that we go back to Durango, and we did. Durango is a very beautiful place, and many people want to live there, so there was no place for us to rent. We found a campground in the nearby mountains and made ourselves a kind of "tent home." Several families had the same idea, so we had "tent neighbors" while we were there.

Since there were so few places available to rent, we found ourselves in town early each morning so we could get the newspaper as it came "hot off of the presses" to see if anything new had come up for rent during the previous day. We had to do it quickly because there were always many people looking. Rentals did not remain vacant very long in Durango.

Finally, we found a three bedroom trailer a little north of Durango. We were just moving in when Rodger joined us; his father had died as he was leaving Oakland and his trip had been delayed for two weeks. Beau and Brian decided to move on. They went to Texas.

Rodger and I loved Durango and soon we both got jobs in a fairly exclusive community just outside the small mountain town of Bayfield, about 15 miles east of Durango. The area consisted of wonderful woods with a scattering of vacation homes and upscale cabins owned by people who wanted to get away from it all. It also boasted a recreation center called Windows on the Woods which had a bar, a restaurant and a swimming pool. I became the bartender and Rodger became the lifeguard at the pool. A lake could be seen from the bar. It was beautiful, reflecting the blue sky with gorgeous white clouds and green Colorado mountains all around.

For the most part, only the people who lived in the immediate area came to the bar. It turned out that many people from the Mafia had homes in the sleepy community. Sometimes in the evening there would be several tall, well-built men, dressed impeccably in very expensive suits, just standing around. I knew that they were bodyguards and that someone of importance in the Mafia was there. My drinks were always mixed very well on those evenings.

Among my regular customers during the day was the Godfather's niece and her husband. I'll call them Bud and Barbara. They were fun. They would come to the bar in the afternoons and we became friends. Many times they would be my only customers and I would invent drinks for them to try. She told me that Bud had to ask the Godfather's permission to marry her.

One day as Rodger and I arrived for work, I found my boss, the manager of the bar, with two of the locals. They were what we called Redneck trouble-makers. I name them Bubba and Jub. I didn't like them very much.

"Cut them off," the boss told me as he left. He had been serving them drinks all morning and they were drunk; not the best situation to walk into. "Give me another drink," Bubba slurred. "How about having a cup of coffee, then I'll give you one," I said, trying to be diplomatic. "Are you cutting me off?" he said. "After I've been paying for drinks all day"?

"You son of a bitch," he said as he stumbled off of the bar stool. He came behind the bar with his fists doubled up. Hate shrouded his face as he came closer to me. I couldn't, and wouldn't run; and I certainly wouldn't fight with him, so I said to myself (over and over), *This is not of my world.* Closer he came. *I am not in his world.* I forced the thought and believed it. Standing still, looking at him with no reaction, I knew that I was in a world different from his. One fist punched out and ended up next to my left ear. The other thrust past and stopped next to my right ear. I neither blinked nor flinched. We just stood there looking at each other. He couldn't hit me. Swearing, he left the bar, tipping over bar stools on his way out. He went into the pool area, threw lounging chairs into the pool, and left. A few days later, I was walking down Durango's Main Street. "Michael," someone yelled. Bubba was across the street, waving at me and smiling. I nodded back and walked on with a grin on my face.

Most of the time business was slow at the bar so I had fun inventing drinks. The "Chocolate Orange Blossom" and the "Girl Scout Cookie," named after the chocolate mint cookie, were my favorites and they tasted much like their names suggested. I also created a blue and white polka dot drink I called, "Colorado Clouds." It was just a frozen lime daiquiri with a layer of blue Curacao dribbled on top. The blue streaked down among the iced drink, making it look like a blue sky with white clouds. I would serve it with a green slice of lime on the edge of the glass and a red straw. Sometimes, when it was slow, I'd send a waiter around just carrying one. He'd get an order for one every time.

At the beginning of the winter, Durango holds what they call Snowdown, consisting of special winter events that culminate in a drink-making contest at some bar in town. The local bartenders enter drinks that they have invented and the winning drink becomes the official Snowdown drink for the season. Usually there is snow and tourists in for the skiing during Snowdown, but this particular year there was no snow. They held Snowdown just the same. I decided to enter my "Colorado Clouds" in the contest. Unfortunately, the bar where they had the contest did not have blue Curacao. Since my drink depended on the blue liqueur to make it special, all the "show" was gone and I was just making a frozen lime daiquiri. I did not win. The drink that did win that year was called, "Yellow snow." The mind reels.

Each drink that was entered was passed around for all of us to taste. I got very drunk as the tasting continued. After the contest was over, I somehow managed to get back to Windows on the Woods. Soon the manager came to me and told me that I really needed to go home. He was right. I agreed, and began to drive home.

As I drove down a dirt road on my way home, a tire blew out. I opened the door and leaned to get out of the truck; only to find myself losing my balance. I fell from the truck and staggered all the way to the other side of the road where I fell down. I could not stand up, so I slowly crawled back to the car and changed the tire while on my knees. Pulling myself back into the truck, I continued to drive home. (I was much too drunk to walk.) Near our trailer, there was a big ditch that ran next to the road. As I neared the trailer; I saw the top of a car in the ditch. *Hmmm, Looks like Rodger's car*, I thought, and it was. It seems he was doing no better at driving than I was at walking. He ran the car off of the road into the ditch and walked home.

Rodger's father had left him some money when he died and we were looking to buy a place of our own. One day we saw an ad in the paper: A three bedroom trailer "as is" for sale about 40 miles away. The price was only $2,000 so we went to see it. The trailer was in the middle of a field; the frame was not straight, but bent in the middle so that the trailer seemed to be split in half and was sitting in the field like an upside down V. The middle was higher than both the front and the back and the outside walls were pushed open where the trailer was bent.

When the trailer was first moved onto the field it had gotten stuck in the mud. A helpful farmer offered to use his tractor to tow it out. For some reason he hooked a chain, not to the front of the trailer, but to the middle. He then began to pull the trailer sideways. The girders of the trailer, being pulled sideways, gave way and bent. The trailer buckled and the walls in the middle pushed outward, exposing the inside of the trailer.

Shooing chickens out of the trailer, Rodger and I checked it out. Other than the floor not being straight (it did make me a bit dizzy to walk on it) and the wall boards in the middle opened to the outside, we figured that we could make it a habitable place to live. Rodger offered the man $1,000 cash. "If it falls apart as we try to tow it home," he said, "we will only loose $1,000. We are taking a chance that we will be able to transport it," Rodger mentioned as he held out $1,000. The man agreed. I doubt that he had any other offers. We had a trailer transport company tow the trailer into Durango. There was no problem at all in moving it into a trailer park south of town. The truck driver told us that it had "tracked perfectly."

I began the task of setting the trailer up as best I could. I knew that it needed to be put up on blocks and off the tires, so I was putting cinder blocks under the framework of the trailer. However, I was not putting the blocks crossways to the girders which would keep it from tipping, but was placidly placing the blocks lengthwise, aligning them with the frame. Somehow, that seemed reasonable to me. I didn't realize it but this would make it very wobbly.

I was placing the last block when there was a mighty crash as the blocks fell over and the entire trailer crashed to the ground. I heard a loud "thud" as I saw the 12 ton trailer strike the ground inches in front of my face. *Holy chit that was close*"!

Rodger, of course, was devastated to see me get "chopped off" by the trailer edging. There was no movement at first, then my legs started to kick. Rodger raced into action and pulled me out.

He was white-faced but we both began to laugh as we looked at our new home. The impact of the trailer hitting the ground had forced the bend out of the girders, straightening them out. The wall boards had snapped back into place and the trailer was perfectly level.

We had to chase the chickens out of the trailer at first. Kind of a scary beginning at best.

It was a give and take chance that the trailer would fall apart on the way back to town, but it made it.

Not much to begin with. But it was a roof over our heads.

With spit, polish and elbow greese,
we made a nice home for us.

We later bought
a delivery van
which we made into
a fun motor home

We were now were
officially trailer trash.
But we were comfortable
and we owned both of
them so no more renting.

Wiping my hands together as with a job-well-done; all I had to do was screw the walls back into place. It was going to be our home and it was just fine. $1,000 for a three bedroom trailer that gave us the new title of Trailer Trash, but we had a home at last. We would sell it three years later for $8,000.

We had found a trailer park just south of town. The trailer park was right next to some beautiful hills, and having a place to live at last, made us very happy. Rodger and I took our dog, Lady, hiking often in the nearby hills. Lady took off by herself one time, and was gone for several days. We were afraid that she had died, but one day she dragged herself back home all puffed up with an infection of some kind. We raced her to the vet and saved her from that, but soon afterwards, she was killed by a truck on the nearby highway.

A dog had become part of our lives by then, and Lady had convinced us that a female Labrador/Golden Retriever mix, with the resulting loyalty, patience and overall personality, was the dog for us. As it happens, when we looked in the paper, we found an ad for free Lab/Golden retriever pups. Of course we went to get one.

We were watching the six pups of the litter, wondering which to choose, when a gust of wind came up and blew a paper bag across the backyard. One of the pups ran after it and jumped in. "That's the one," I said. Thus, we acquired Maggie; without a doubt, the best dog I've ever had.

Rodger, Maggie and I loved to go hiking along the Animas, a beautiful river that runs down through the Animas canyon and through Durango. There are cliffs to climb, places to swim, and beautiful trees lining its banks. Once while we were hiking, Rodger picked Maggie up and, just for the heck of it, threw her into the river. While I didn't quite understand his reasoning, I laughed along with him as Maggie shook herself off and ran on. I didn't see Maggie for a while, but at one point in our hike, we came upon a hill growing up from the river bank. Maggie was running down the hill as fast as she could go. She took a great leap and hit Rodger right in the chest, pushing him into the river. We all laughed with Maggie joining in. What a great dog!

A little farther up the trail, we came upon a cliff. I wanted to climb it to see what was on top. "Come on, Maggie," I said. "Let's go climb the cliff." She ran to the cliff and started to climb. She was a very good climber, and the cliff was fairly steep. Nearing the top, we came upon a place where she couldn't get a footing. I was climbing right behind her. She just looked back at me, letting me know that she needed a push. I gave her a shove, and we made it to the top.

Maggie loved to climb. I even taught her to climb trees, if they leaned just a bit to one side. Whenever she saw a tree that was growing at an angle, Maggie would climb it. Again I say, "what a great dog she was." She loved people, us, other dogs and life itself.

Now that we had our trailer and our dog, we wanted to find some gay friends. People we had met while we were camping in the mountains introduced us to a lesbian named Becky, who was a student at Fort Luis College. Soon we were invited to a small gay party at the college. Becky took a liking to me and my "big city" thinking. "Why don't you start a gay club?" she asked. Before the end of the evening the "Four Corners Human Awareness Group" (affectionately called FCHAG for short) was conceived. (The Four corners is where Colorado, Utah, Nevada and New Mexico come together. It's the only place in the nation where four states join.)

We began our club by organizing a combined beer bust and potluck dinner to be held in the mountains not far from where we had camped when we first arrived in Durango. We passed out Xeroxed flyers to people who we knew were gay. On our flyer we had three sets of symbols: male/male, female/female and male/female symbols. This was our only reference to alternate sexuality. On the bottom of the flyer it said: "This comes from a friend, please pass it along to a friend."

We had 54 people at our first beer bust and potluck party. At one point, I took a deep breath and asked in a loud voice for everyone to form a circle around me. I told them that we wanted to create a club where gay and gay friendly people could come together for fun and growth. We were planning to have dances, parties, rap sessions, potluck dinners and picnics. We also planned to speak at various places to let others know about gay people. Our idea was to help gays and lesbians feel comfortable with themselves in a community that openly detested them. We also wanted to help straight people who might want to learn about the gay community.

So, with hot dogs and a keg of beer, the Four Corners Human Awareness Group was formed. A few years later we were to have about 175 members from the four adjoining states. We also printed a bi-monthly newsletter called "The Four Corners Echo." It contained information from other gay groups within the four state area, plus our own get-togethers, community outreach, rap sessions, political situations and gossip.

Our rap sessions were open-ended and gave people a platform to be able to discuss situations that were bothering them. Since most of our group could not be open about their sexuality, the sessions became a kind of group therapy.

Once, while we were having a rap session, someone told me that there was a guy outside who was listening at the window. I went out to him, put my arms around him, and invited him to join us. It was difficult for him even to be there; to admit to others that he had gay tendencies and he could not join with the group. He just asked me to tell him that he wasn't bad. He also asked us to please keep sending the Four Corners Echo to him. Then he left, saying he'd come back but he never did.

We had some dances at a Catholic church in Shiprock, New Mexico. One of the churches' Brothers was a member of our group, and the priest was supportive as well. There was a youth group at the church that selected different topics they wanted to explore, and once a month the priest would get an authority on the topic to talk with the kids. One of the topics they wanted to know more about was gays. This was a perfect opportunity for us to help educate some children who would grow up knowing about gay people. Six of us went to speak to the class. Our plan was to tell something about ourselves as individuals, then to open it up for questions from the group. I think we were as astonished as the kids, to find how different our responses were.

We were also invited to speak to a youth group at the Methodist, Indian mission in Aztec, New Mexico. After telling a bit about ourselves, we opened it up for questions. You could have heard a pin drop because they were too shy to ask. So we passed around some paper and pencils and let them write their questions. A week later, I received a card from them that I have kept ever since. On the front it said, "No greater strength than gentleness, no greater gentleness than true strength," an Indian proverb. Inside, of course, all the students had signed.

Twice; we were invited to speak to groups at Fort Louis College in Durango. We were comfortable with our roles in the panels by then and had included people from as many differing backgrounds as we could find to add variety to our discussions. We had both gay and lesbian couples, single and bi-sexual people and even a transsexual person at one point.

During this time I was also acting with a group called Durango Lively Artists." They had conducted auditions for the play *Wait Until Dark*. With my background in the Renaissance Faire and the Buddy & Mike show, I felt that I stood a very good chance of getting a part. I did, as Carlino, one of the policemen. I had to put on my own make-up. I didn't have a clue how to do it. Everyone was too busy putting their own "faces" on to help, so I wasn't able to get any help or directions. I never did learn to do it very well, but I guess my acting made up for it. My role was small, but I got good reviews.

During the next season I tried out for Dr. Einstein in the play, *Arsenic and Old Lace*. I had played a small part in the same play when I was in High school. "Dr. Einstein" had used a pseudo Germanic accent that was very effective. I did my cold reading using that accent. They were impressed and I got the part. In the six weeks leading up to the production, the local paper ran a small bio ad about each of the actors. They did not include one about me. I was offended and told the producer as much. I was told that it was simply because all the other actors had been with the company longer than I had.

I put my heart into the part of Dr. Einstein. At one point, I had to run off the stage because the police were coming. I went to the theater early to perfect running directly toward the audience until it looked as if I were about to leap off of the stage, but at the last minute (and the last few inches of stage), I pivoted with an upraised leg, to run off to stage right, as the scene called for.

I also talked an actor, who played the part of a policeman, into changing one of his lines so that I could get an extra laugh. He played the part of a dumb cop who couldn't figure out that he was looking for me and my partner. In the scene, he was on the phone repeating a description of me. As Dr. Einstein, I was bent over a table signing a piece of paper but listening to the policeman as he was repeating my description. The script had him reading my statistics as height, weight, age, color of hair, etc. I had him change my height to the last place in the list.

As it became obvious that he was describing me, I straightened slowly from my writing, to stand at my full height, listening to the cop and thinking that I had been discovered. "Yup, Sergeant, I've got that," he said. "Fiftyish, brown hair, brown eyes, 150 pounds, 5'10" tall." When he said, "5'10" tall," I immediately bent my knees, to appear shorter. The audience roared.

When the performance was over, I got a standing ovation;

applause even greater than the play itself received. The reviews about me in the paper were stunning as well, and I felt avenged for the missing bio during the weeks before the production.

While we did *Arsenic and Old Lace*, we at the Four Corners Awareness group were asked to speak at Fort Louis College again. I invited all the actors from the play to come hear us. The local health clinician, a fellow actor, was there. He treated the local VD cases and he also knew that I was gay.

There were seven or eight on our panel-people who were male, female, white and a Native American woman who was the daughter of the chief of the tribe, (I suspect he was called a Chairman, but she called him a Chief). There were two gay male couples, a lesbian couple, and a guy and a lady who was single. We sat in the auditorium and shared a bit about ourselves: "I was born a Mormon in Utah." "I was married and have a daughter." "I'm Catholic." "My father is the chief of the tribe."

After we told about ourselves, we asked the audience for questions. We were prepared to answer anything they wanted to ask. The questions were always answered differently by each of us, showing that we were individuals and not meant to be lumped into one group. One of the first questions to be asked was from my fellow actor and health agent who jumped up and asked, "Is it true that gay men have more casual sex than straight men?"

"It's true for Rodger and me," I said, "but I can't speak for Alan and Dan." Alan and Dan said that they were monogamous.

There were as many different answers as there were people. I think people were influenced with our talks. Before they met us, most thought that gay people were "out there somewhere," not people they knew or interacted with everyday. With our talks, people could learn that we were all individuals with different lives and different feelings, no longer grouped as a "them."

It turns out there was a serial killer within our group. His name was Eli. He had left his Amish family in Pennsylvania where he had murdered his wife then burned the barn down around her. Then, he had taken his small son and left. He came to Durango, partnered with one of our members, and joined FCHAG. I have some pictures of him taken at a Halloween party; one with Rodger and others with the group of FCHAG friends in costume. I also have some pictures with his arm around Ken, who he later stabbed to death.

One day Rodger and I saw a long house trailer being towed into town. It had been built as a portable spa, Jacuzzi and steam room, and was available to be rented out for parties. When we learned what it was, Rodger said, "Let's reserve it for New Year's Eve, now!" So the day it rolled into town we reserved it for the "Giant FCHAG New Year's Eve Bash." Then we started planning.

As the end of the year approached, several groups clamored to rent the spa trailer for their own parties, but were disappointed to find that it had already been reserved. One can only guess as to the reactions if it were known that a gay group had beat them to the punch.

Sometime in the fall, Rodger and I bought a log house closer to town on a quarter acre of ground; a much more respectable address and a better place for our year-end celebration. We were moving up in the world.

People came from Utah, Nevada, New Mexico and Colorado for the party. The event was a huge success and the spa itself was the star of the show, as people rushed down the pathway through the snow to soak in the warm water with each other.

Eli, the murderer, was there with his partner. A month or so later, Eli sneaked away while also stealing a prize stallion. He ended up in Texas. There was a story in Readers Digest called "Little Boy Blue." People in the Texas town had found a little boy dead in a culvert, dressed neatly in blue pajamas but partially eaten by wolves. The child was Eli's son. Eli came back to Durango to kill Ken, as I mentioned. He dumped his body in a dumpster and wrote, "Queer" on the side of it in blood. He was eventually caught, and a book was written about him called, *Abandoned Prayers*. Our club and our party were mentioned in the book.

Maggie in her favorite place, sitting on a limb of a tree.

And again as she looks out over a cliff into Yosemite.

Chapter 14

Back to California and another life begins ... again

Rodger and I had moved to Durango, Colorado. Without intending to do it we formed a gay club that covered the Four Corners Area. Through the club we had helped many people, both gay and straight, to see the LGBT community with different eyes. While we felt that we had settled down, another life was waiting in the wings.

It is not always the best idea to just give people much money. In later years, Rodger and I figured that between us, we went through $250,000 in the four years that we were partners. Both of our parents had died and left us money; I had also received some money from the government because of being paralyzed. We had no idea how to handle the money, however. At one point, Rodger would ask if I had any change. What he meant, was if I had anything less than a twenty dollar bill. Fortunately we learned our lesson.

We spent and spent until one day I happened to balance the check book, more out of boredom than anything. I found that we had exactly $25 left in the bank. "Rodger," I said. "We're broke." Interestingly, neither of us panicked. We decided to spend the remaining $25 on a party and spend all of it to make room for more money to come in.

A day or so after the party, Rodger got a job at a hospice and I got a job at Panhandler Pies, a restaurant that specialized in chicken and pies. We had made friends with the owner over the past year or so and the chicken dinners were great. Sitting with the owner over coffee one afternoon, someone told her that the dishwasher had just quit. Since I needed a job, I offered to work as a dishwasher for her in exchange for learning how to cook. "But never make the mistake of thinking that I am a dishwasher," I told her.

We fell back into the habit of working again without any stress at all. Living within a budget wasn't a problem for us either. We were easy-going about things. It didn't take us long to begin saving money. This time it meant more to us since we had earned it instead of having it given to us.

We also found an older delivery van. It was a 28 foot long Astro Chief delivery van. There were only a few of them made. I wanted to make it into a motor home for us because we were planning to take it to California while acting in the Renaissance Faire; plus, both of us liked to travel and wanted to meander in comfort.

Then one day I got a call. "It's your mother," the voice said.

Jerry, her husband, my step-father, had just died. She had to get my telephone number from my Aunt Ruby. She asked if I would come to her. It had been many years since my mother had disowned me. "No, I won't come," I replied. Rodger wanted us to go. He wanted to meet the family that I had left behind, so we ended up going to Salt Lake City. It was the first time I'd seen my mother in many years. First they dis-owned me, then I disowned them. Family had not been my strong suit so far.

Later, my mother visited us in Durango. This was the first time she had ever visited me in a home of my own. She loved our van and made it into a bedroom for herself.

During one of her visits to Durango, our friends Alan and Danny had us over for dinner. They were friends from FCHAG, and had served on several panel discussions with us. Alan and I shared a mutual interest in photography. Durango is a beautiful place and both of us shot many rolls of film. We would scour the nearby mountains for beautiful shots, then we would have dinner parties and show slides of our recent work. Sometimes a few of our friends would show pictures as well, but Alan and I were the ones who were most involved with them. Whenever we had a dinner party, our slide shows became the desert.

I began to noticed that there was something different with my pictures. I had acquired an SLR camera with an 80 to 200 mm zoom lens by that time, which opened up a whole new world of photography for me. Being able to control my exposure combined with the ability to zoom in or out, made all the difference.

Mother, Rodger and I had a wonderful time with Alan and Danny and I'm sure we did a slide show of our work. As we were driving back to the trailer my mother said to me, "Michael, you are so loved." This from a mother who hadn't really loved me. The following morning we were talking over breakfast and she said, "Michael, you're a religious man, I want to ask you something."

"Hell," I said, "I'm not religious." To which she replied,

"Michael, you are the most religious man I've ever met." Spiritual is the word that she should have used, but it was more than enough. My mother had "seen" me at last. Then she went home and soon died. Nevertheless, she got to know the person that I had become, and I got to know her as well.

Soon after my mother died, I got a call from the costume director at the Renaissance faire. She wanted me to work in the costume department at the faire for the coming season. She told me that I had already been "auditioned" and the job was mine.

The last time I had acted in the faire, I had left a night shirt behind. I had sewn the night shirt by hand, and had made a night cap to match as well. I made them as a costume for a skit that I had created for the prior year's faire. At night, during the time I was making the costume and dream-planning the skit to come, I would wake myself up laughing as I planned what to do in what I called "The Night Shirt Run." In the skit, there would be a girl who was a "light skirt." My character; Styx, would want to be with her, but she charged a penny. Styx would not have the penny but would tell her that he would pay her after he had his way with her. When he did not have the penny to give her she would take his clothes for payment, then run away with me chasing close behind.

The faire ground is a very large place with many things happening at once. All of a sudden, out of the crowd, came a woman running with her arms full of clothes followed closely by me in my night shirt and cap, crying "Please give me back my clothes." I was not wearing shoes or anything besides the night shirt and cap for that matter, as I hobbled pitifully behind her. Often, I would stop to rub a toe that had been stubbed on the rocks of the road. It was a hilarious but exhausting skit to do and the stubbed toes were more often than not, real. Sometimes she would stop so we could catch our breath. A crowd would gather around us and we would tell our story to the laughing people. I would beg the people watching us to help me get my clothes back. Then we would run on into the faire to continue the same skit somewhere else.

A fellow actor had wanted to borrow the night shirt at one point and I had forgotten to take it with me when I returned to Colorado. The actor was the costume director's boyfriend and she liked the work I had done on my night shirt, so she was offering me a job.

Rodger was as excited as I was to go to the faire. Rodger loved life, and if anything new or different was offered, he was all for it. Since we would be in California for at least six months we decided to make our van into a motor home. It was just a delivery truck but I figured that I could make it into a comfortable home for us to live.

When my mother died, I got some money from the estate so we could afford to buy whatever was needed for our new motor home. I began building a bathroom, a bedroom, some closets, and a kitchen. Then we got separate (and comfortable) driver and passenger seats that swiveled so we could turn them around to create a living room.

I was building some cupboards and cutting some wood. It was a long piece and I had Rodger hold one end up for me. At one point, Rodger sneezed and got distracted. The wood caught in the blade and so did my fingers. Two of my fingers had been cut off and held on only with skin and some tissue. I grabbed my fingers with my other hand and we raced to the hospital. As it happens, there was a very good hand surgeon at the hospital who sewed my fingers back on. I did lose the use of the end joint in both fingers, but he managed to save the fingers for me. It took a month or so before I had use of my hand again, but I was able to get a lot done without it.

As with most clubs and organizations only a small percentage of the people do the actual work. The Four Corners Human Awareness Group was no exception. Since I knew that Rodger and I were to leave Durango, I tried to get others interested in running our club.

Then we bought a van to travel in.

Like the trailer, it wasn't much to look at inside.

But with a little work, it turned out just fine.

I resigned as Chairman of FCHAG, offering to help as I could until we left. It worked for a while as Alan took over and even published an edition of "The Four Corners Echo," our newsletter. The vision for the club had been mostly mine, so when we left, try though he might, there was really not very much that Alan could do to keep the club on course. Not too long after that, the club was no more.

Nonetheless we could look back on what we had accomplished with our group. All of us had made friends that we hadn't known were gay or gay friendly before, and most of the gay people in the area felt a lot better about who and what they were than they did before we had our discussion groups. People in town and in various churches who had thought of gays and lesbians as perverted at best, learned that we were "just folks" much like themselves. We left many people behind, carrying a very different perspective of us than they had before we came and we felt that our job was done.

When we left Durango, I moved "full force" into my new life, leaving many friends and a whole way of life behind. There are few people that I have remained in communication with as I have changed from one life to another. I get to know too many people, and keeping in touch with the past as I venture into the future has always been difficult for me. It's like dying and being reborn into a new life.

So Rodger and I were off to California again, this time to work at the Renaissance faire. I had made the van into a comfortable little motor home for us. We were to live in it off and on for several years. It had a full kitchen, and a working bathroom complete with a shower. Our bedroom was a separate room by itself and we carried our own water, white, gray and brown. Life as they say, was good.

I was to work for the costume department for about eight months, working for both the southern California faire during the spring and the northern faire in the fall. Of course all of us in the costume department also acted in the faire so when the faire opened, I was able to act with them again.

Rodger had no problem getting accepted into the faire community and played the part as a duck seller. Somewhere he had found four tiny ducklings and used our dog Maggie as a duck herder.

It was fun and Maggie loved the faire, to say nothing about all the attention she got. She even had her own pass to the Faire and played her part to perfection.

Poor Styx, created to be a debonair and suave thief, had fallen down a 40 foot cliff and broken his arm as he tried to make a name for himself. You wouldn't think things could get much lower for him but one day Rodger threw the remains of a beer in my crotch, and yelled, "You've pissed your pants." And though I tried to deny it, Styx, already a klutz, became a piss pants as well.

Since I was working for the costume department I made Styx a pair of pants that I lined in yellow, "Lined by his aunt just in case," and I also made them too big, with a snap that held them on. When I pushed with my stomach, the snap would release and the pants would fall down. I worked out many ways where I could get people to help me pull my pants up, (like getting tied up by the Sheriff with my arms around a pole). Styx the piss pants and fool who couldn't keep his pants up, was even more fun to play.

When the six weeks of Southern Faire was over it was time to move up to Novato, north of San Francisco. Rodger's ducks had grown from cute little ducklings into large full size ducks which we carried with us and Maggie in the motor home. Four ducks in a van for any time at all is a very dirty situation, by the way.

We took our time driving up north. One time we stopped at a campground for the night. I opened the door and got out, followed by Rodger and a hitch hiker that we had picked up. Maggie was followed by four large ducks quacking loudly. We were quite a sight and at least one camper packed up and left.

Working in the costume department, I was able to make a night shirt and night cap for Rodger, and together we did the night shirt run. This skit was played in a different way. We both wanted the girl, but we only had a penny between us, so I would go first, have my way with her, then say I had to go and pee and Rodger would take my place. She found out, of course, and ran away carrying all of our clothes. Rodger and I both ran after her, limping bare footed through the fairgrounds. There were a lot of rocks on the way and we didn't have to pretend to stumble and grab at our feet as we ran. I liked playing with Rodger, Maggie and the ducks as well. It was a fun time.

During the six weeks leading up to the opening of the faire, there were rehearsals. At that time they cast for various shows that are put on all over the fairgrounds as well as the variety of well known characters with which the faire abounds. I tried out for a part in a production of Hamlet, produced by the Reduced Shakespeare Company. It was done as a comedy. We did the play in 25 minutes which in itself made it hilarious, but as an encore (which we always got), we did the play in five minutes. If the audience continued to clap (as they always did), we did the play in one minute. It was riotous and we got rave reviews in the San Francisco Examiner.

I was having so much fun playing the role of Styx, I rarely played the part of Michael the valet anymore. Since Styx was well known at the faire, it was as Styx that I acted in Hamlet, playing the parts of Horatio, the ghost and the king.

This was the last time that I was to act with the faire. Life moved on and when the faire was over we would return to Durango. We wanted this to be a special trip for us so we planned to take three or four weeks to get home. I had some finishing touches to do with the water system in the van, so after the faire closed we moved into a campground on the Russian River for a week or so while I completed the work.

We took a trip up along the coast to Washington, then

followed the Columbia River before ending up in Durango. A strange thing happened with that trip; as we started out from the campground it began to rain. It rained every day during the three weeks or so of our travels. As we entered Durango the rain stopped. A sign? Perhaps.

The van made it very easy to pick up and go. Gas was cheap and both Rodger and I had money. We did a lot of wandering around the West, going deep into New Mexico, all around Colorado and back to California several times. Life in Durango and with each other, had become fairly routine, and before long one of us would take off in the van and go to Tucson, Arizona for a few weeks while the other stayed behind in Durango. Soon Rodger decided to move back to Los Angeles. We were no longer partners, yet it was not long after he left that I moved there as well. I lived in the motor home for several years. It was just right for one person. Rodger and I were still friends but not living together anymore.

I was visiting some friends from the faire who invited me to a party of "faire folk." They were, indeed, like a family. While I was there I was introduced to a guy whose name was also Michael Fleming. I said, "I'm Michael Fleming too."

"Are you THE Michael Fleming?" he asked. I have to admit that I had made a name for myself at the Faire and it was great to know that they still talked about me. I knew that I had given my heart to the Faire. His statement let me know that it was worth it.

Now that I was back in Los Angeles, I decided to pursue the interest that I had developed in photography while in Durango. I always wondered what it was about my photographs that was different, so I decided to settle down for a time and take some photography classes. Rodger took them, too. We both loved photography. I soon found what was different about my pictures was that I had an "eye" for composition. I had taken several thousand pictures while in Durango. After my first class I threw half the pictures away. After my second class I threw half away again. Soon, I was left with only the "cream of the crop." With these slides I created a class on composition. As it happens, the school ended up hiring me and I worked at Los Angeles City College for 12 years. I now had a job that I liked in an area that I liked as well, so I bought a home north of Los Angeles and settled down.

Since I was working in a school atmosphere; I began taking night classes for fun. I came to realize that I only needed a few credits to get myself a degree. I didn't need one, but why not? So I started taking the courses still remaining to get an AA degree. I needed an English course and found how much I love writing. My teacher gave me AA+ for my work. That made me feel confident so I registered for Astronomy to fulfill the natural sciences requirement.

In the first class, the teacher told us of a total eclipse of the sun that would be happening over the Big Island of Hawaii on July 11, 1991. Thinking of the song, *You're so vain, you probably think this song is about you*, I allowed the words, *Then you flew to Nova Scotia to see the total eclipse of the sun*, to run through my head. *I can do this*, I thought and by the time I got home I knew that I was going to Hawaii to photograph the total eclipse of the sun.

I went to Hawaii with my friend Jim. We spent the first day touring the island with a rented convertible. Both of us were nudists so we planned to spend the night before the eclipse sleeping on the nude portion of Honokohau Harbor Beach and enjoying the wonderful warmth of the evening,

The Big Island was preparing for an influx of tourists coming to watch the eclipse. As evening approached, rangers patrolled and cleared the beaches of any lingering tourists so people were forced to sleep in a hotel.

Nude beaches for privacy, are typically located at the most

remote places on a beach and the rangers did not make it out to the nude area. So while others were packed into crowded hotels, we enjoyed an evening with about 20 other scattered nudists, sleeping on the sand with the gentle lapping sound of the ocean in the background.

The morning dawned dark and cloudy. Low and heavy roiling clouds filled the sky above our heads. We had only moments left before the eclipse was to occur. *I did not come here to be clouded out*, I thought. I raised my camera and pointed to where the sun was beginning to darken as the moon started to pass in front. As I focused my camera, the clouds began to part, allowing a small opening between me and the eclipsing sun. When the eclipse was over and I had finished photographing the event, the clouds closed over and the day was overcast again. Later we heard that the tourists at the King Kamaymayha Hotel, not too far away across a bit of water, had to run to watch the eclipse on huge monitors that had been provided just in case there were low clouds.

When I got back to the lab at school, I developed the film and discovered that after the clouds had parted, in the few minutes of light before the darkness of the eclipse, the clouds took on life-like, constantly changing forms. Beginning with what looked like to me, a giant hand reaching out and pushing the clouds back with the eclipsing sun sitting in the palm of the hand. Then the clouds changed into three distinct face forms, two old ladies and the profile of a child at the edge of the opening.

It takes some imagination to see the hand and the faces. These are, after all, clouds. They are there however, for those who can see. I call the hand picture "And the hand of God opened - -." The face pictures I call, "The Holy Family at the Birth."

Since the clouds were so low and turbulent, I knew that other than those at the top of Mauna Kea, only we who were naked on that lonely end of the nude beach, had been able to see the event first hand.

I printed all the photographs without editing them. Later, at home, I noticed one with a streak of light in it. Thinking of an old American Indian tradition of making an intentional flaw in some of their works: *Only the Great Spirit can make something perfect,* they felt. I decided that the streak was a distortion in the film and I destroyed that frame only to find later that it was the beginning spark of light from the "diamond ring effect" perfectly aligning itself with the "eye" of what I thought was the profile of the child. It was the "perfect" shot. Fortunately I had printed it before throwing it away.

The clouds begin to part, revealing the eclipse for me

Note: Originally the photographs were taken upside down.
It was only after accidentally checking a negative sideways that I found the faces and the hand.

The Hand begins to form

- - And the hand of God opened.

(If you turn the page to the right
you can see the faces begin to form).

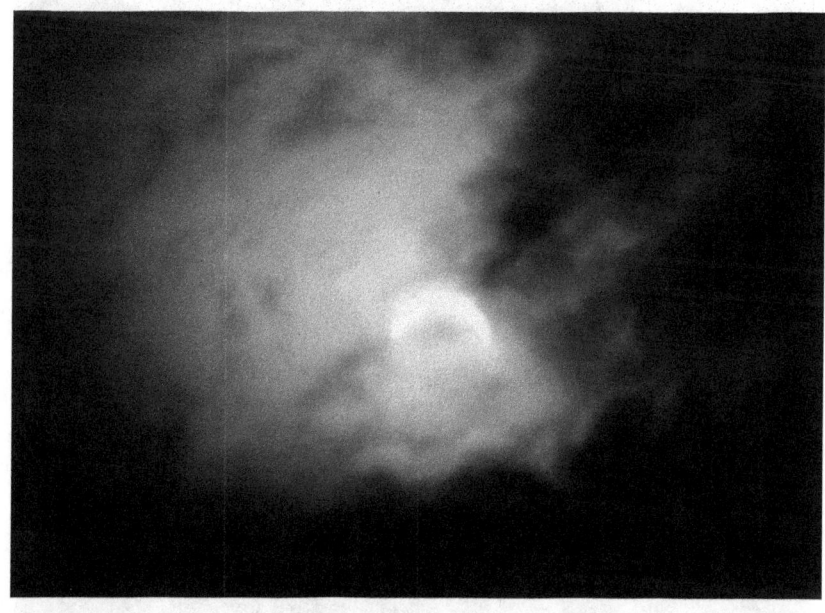

The Holy Family at the Birth

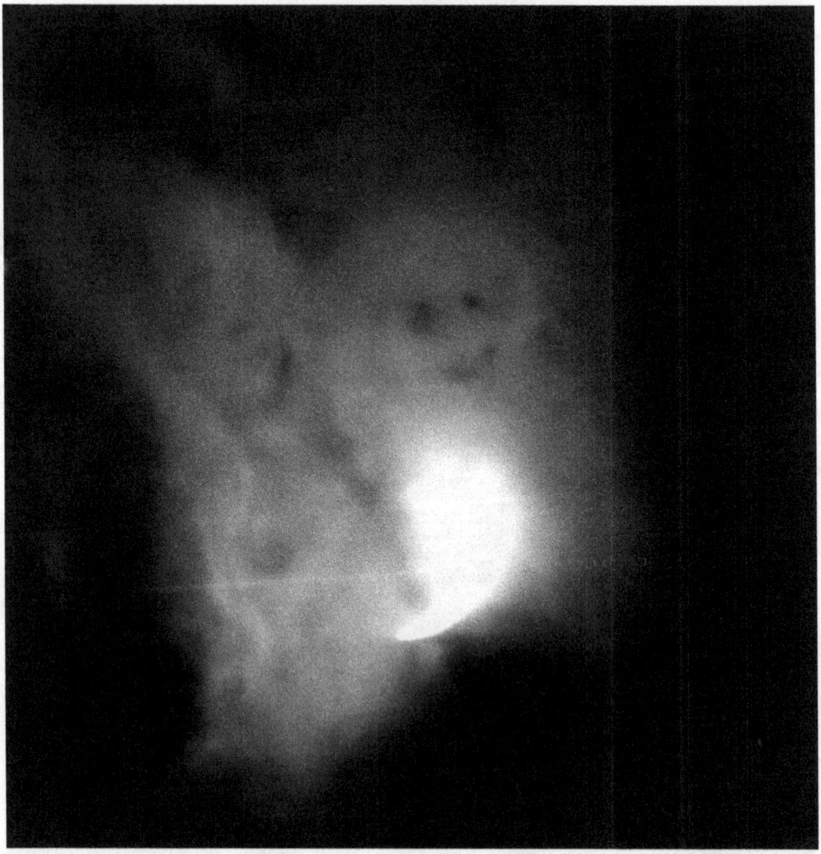

And the eclipse

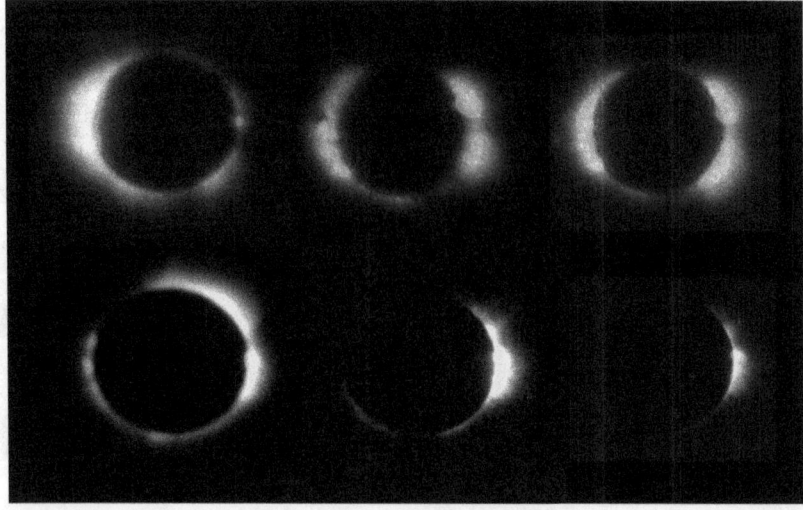

Time passed.

The learning cycle of my ruling planet Saturn takes about 28 years, give or take a couple of years, either way. At the completion of the first cycle I became a hippie. Now I was at the point of the completion of the second cycle. I decided that I would retire from the college on my 56th birthday to begin the second cycle of my life aligned with Saturn.

I told one of the teachers, who I admired and trusted, of my intent. He responded with shock. "You can't do that," he told me. "You have a good job and you're secure." I was shaken by his lack of confidence and asked for a few days off to contemplate my decision. To sort things out for myself, I went to Sedona, Arizona; considered a very spiritual place. Sedona is surrounded by mountains, and as I began to descend to the town itself I saw a sign pointing to a scenic view turnout at the side of the road. I decided to come back to shoot the view point with the breaking of the morning sun when I returned home.

I spent several days taking photographs along the river in Sedona trying to make up my mind about whether or not to retire. My mind was still not made up as I began my final day in Sedona. I was a bit disappointed that I had not solved the dilemma of quitting my job, but I had the goal of reaching the top of the mountain to photograph the view point at the break of dawn.

It was dark when I woke up but I was able to find a cup of coffee somewhere. I was racing to make it to the top of the mountain by daybreak. It took longer than I thought, and as I found the turnout I could see that the sky was beginning to brighten.

I grabbed my camera bags and tripod and ran toward the view point. I was afraid I would not be able to reach it in time. Running pointedly ahead, I did not look to my left or my right.

As I ran I heard a voice say,

"I'm ready for my close up, Mr.DeMille."[1] Off to my left, the sun was just clearing the top of the mountain, light rays were shining through pine trees in the early morning fog sending diamond shaped shadows tumbling down the mountain side. What a glorious sight it was. I shot a whole series of pictures, until the sun had cleared the mountain and the mist began to clear. The actual view point was just a large cliff that jutted out from the side of the mountain. The viewpoint that nature had provided for me was far superior.

Again, my own pathway had lead me away from the travelled road to find a treasure. I was left with the feeling that I had to follow my own pathway. I knew then that it was right for me to retire as planned. I returned to Los Angeles ready to end another chapter in my unfolding life.

What beautiful visions awated my camera

---
1 An often quoted line from the movie, "Sunset Boulevard."

"I'm ready for my close-up Mr. DeMille."

The rising sun, the mist and the trees themselves combined to give me my own special view point.

Everywhere I looked, there was fantasyland.

And finally, the actual view point.

Chapter 15

Return to the Redwoods

A teacher at Los Angeles City College told me that I moved more than anyone he had ever met. Looking back on my life I have to agree with him. When I came back to California and finally settled down, I made a new life with new friends, and different goals. My interest in photography and travel often combined to find me on the road with my dogs and my camping gear.

Having the motor home, combined with our travels to act in the Renaissance Faire and our trips around the South West, instilled in me a love of travel. My favorite places to go were the gold mining areas of Northern California, the Redwoods, and visiting Aunt Ruby in Fallon, Nevada. Fallon had since replaced Salt Lake City as my destination of choice. Somehow I found not only the money to do it, but the time to do it as well. I travelled a lot during this period of my life.

Often I would drive to Fallon just for a few days, to see and help Aunt Ruby. She was growing older and I wanted to spend as much time with her as I could.

Once when I was on my way to Fallon, I noticed beautiful shadow patterns winding their way down the side of some oil tanks that lined a portion of the highway. I stopped and took some pictures of them. When I got back to the lab at school and printed the pictures, I realized that I should have used a telephoto lens. The shadows and tanks were just too small for the effect that I had wanted.

Spring break was coming up and I was determined to return to Fallon to shoot the shadow patterns on the oil tanks using a long lens. I also decided that I wanted to take a portrait of Aunt Ruby as well. So I loaded my truck with the photo equipment that I would need for both shoots.

When I got to the oil tanks, I saw that the shadows were not at all what I had seen before. This was the second time in my photographic career that I was shown the lesson that the sun changes positions as seasons pass, and lighting is only repeated at similar times of the year. I would have to return to Fallon at the same time of year as when I had first taken the shots if I were to get the effect that I wanted. I did do this, and months later on a return trip, I got some wonderful pictures.

Another lesson that I learned (and keep learning), is that like the sun and shadows cast, life does not repeat itself. This current situation will never come again. One cannot take advantage of this moment tomorrow.

Meanwhile, I got to Fallon to find Aunt Ruby not at her

best. She was getting more frail and weak as the years passed. I set up my photo equipment in the front room while she sat at her kitchen table putting up her hair. I set up a background and lights, then put her favorite chair in front of the background. When her hair was ready, Aunt Ruby came and sat in her chair. We just chatted and I photographed her as we talked.

I got a beautiful picture of her. For her Christmas present that year I gave an 8X10 of the picture to whoever she wanted to have a remembrance of her. It was a wonderful gift, and timely, for it was to be her last Christmas.

On my way back to Los Angeles I decided to drive along the top of the Sierra Nevada Mountain range. It was late at night, and the engine started to die for some reason. I was going down a long slope of a mountain when the truck died. So I turned the motor off, put it in low gear and let it coast a second, then "popped the clutch," causing the motor to resume power. The truck kept dying however, and I had to "jump start" it several times on my way down the hill. It wasn't long before I noticed that I was nearing the bottom of the hill. At the bottom, it turned into a long slope climbing back to the top.

I had about three feet to go before reaching the bottom of the hill. This would be my last chance to get the truck going if I was to make it out of the mountains before morning. The road had no traffic at all at that time of night and I knew I would be stranded there if it didn't work this time. I stopped the truck, got out, looked at the darkened sky and said, "Your turn."

Then I got back in the truck and jump started it again. The truck started and continued to run. It kept running all the way up the hill. About a mile away from the top was a motel. I pulled into the motel as the truck died again in their driveway. The motel happened to belong to two lesbians and we bonded immediately.

In the morning I found that the generator belt had broken. Again, I was able to fix my truck with a trusty wire clothes hanger. At the risk of being repetitious, things were more simple then.

Maggie, my constant traveling companion, was getting older and I wanted to get another dog to be her friend, but also to take her place when she died, as I knew she was going to do. I found Sandy, another Lab/Golden retriever female, at the pound. She was sitting very primly in the middle of the cage, looking like she simply didn't know why she was there.

Again, it was love at first sight, and I took her out to meet Maggie. I let Maggie out of the truck to allow her to "discover" Sandy. They played together a bit so I knew they would not fight. Maggie enjoyed playing with the pup but was not at all happy when she realized that she was going to go home with us. As I urged Sandy into the truck, Maggie spread herself out on the seat of the truck to take up all the room. As far as Maggie was concerned, this was her part of the seat and she wasn't sharing with this pup. Sandy, not knowing what else to do, simply sat on top of Maggie all the way home.

It didn't take too long for them to become friends, however, especially since I was working at school and was gone a good part of each day. When I got home from work, I would take the dogs and go hiking in Griffith Park. Maggie, wanting to show off, would climb any tree that was leaning a little bit. This would drive Sandy crazy, and she would bark at Maggie trying to get her to stop. Sandy obviously didn't think dogs should do that. Of course Maggie would climb the next tree, just to tease her.

My dogs were great traveling companions and I was itching to get back to the Redwoods. I made several trips to the Redwoods over the years; mostly to photograph the ancient giants, but also to walk among them and discover the ever changing world in which they live.

I generally made the trip in two days; always stopping at the Russian River in Guerneville so I could spend a day at one of the nude beaches there. The Russian River area is located within a young redwood forest (not old enough yet to be giants). My dogs loved the woods and the water as much as I did.

Refreshed after a day on the riverbank, we would travel farther north to camp within the giant redwoods.

On what was to be the last trip to the redwoods for Maggie and the first trip for Sandy, we stopped at the Russian River, camped, and went off to the nude beach hidden away in the forest at the river's edge.

There was a wonderful spring flowing into a rock-built basin for horses to drink from, located a ways into the forest from the river. We loved to walk within the cool shade of the adjoining redwoods; to drink from the spring, and take a quick dip in the very cold water.

Maggie was fine initially. Later in the day when I wanted to go to the spring again, I noticed that she was a bit worn from the heat of the day and that she was slowing down on our walk. Half way to the spring there was a tree that had fallen across the pathway. On our first trip to the spring both dogs had easily jumped over it. Now it was later in the day and Maggie was tired, but she felt she had to keep up with Sandy. Sandy, still a pup, jumped the tree again with no problem. Maggie only had the energy to jump half way. She bumped into the tree and fell to the ground. I tried to pick her up and carry her over the tree but she refused. The tree had stopped falling about a foot above the pathway so I tried to push Maggie underneath, but again she refused.

Instead, she walked around a bit and noticed some smaller trees that had fallen in cross hatch patterns off to the side of the pathway: this is not uncommon in a redwood forest. She studied these trees for a moment, then carefully climbing onto one of them, began to walk along the top of the trees like a tight-rope walker. She made her way from tree to tree until she zigzagged her way back to the path on the other side of the blocking tree. Maggie was, indeed, quite a dog.

I found myself again in a time of death and transition. Maggie was dying of cancer and I had to put her down. I was broken hearted, but she knew and accepted what was happening.

Rodger and I took her to the vet. She could barely walk so I carried her in, trying to hold back the tears. Waiting to be called, we sat down. I was holding Maggie and stroking her. Someone came in with a puppy and placed it on the floor. Maggie struggled and kicked and wanted to get onto the floor. She hobbled over to the puppy and sniffed at it. When we were called, Maggie refused to be picked up and walked into the room by herself. I looked her in her eyes as they put her to sleep.

My friend Kent was living with me again. He had AIDS, and was in the process of dying. We talked a lot about his impending death, exploring the possibilities and implications between us, trying to help prepare him for his transition. I told him about the tree that had fallen and was decaying at one end while growing new life from the giant roots. I also told him of the trees that I had seen years earlier growing in a circled community with each other. Kent was afraid of dying, afraid that his soul would not "reach out and grow." He wanted to be cremated, and I offered to take his ashes to the center of these trees. "Surrounded by these growing giants, your soul can't help but want to grow," I told him. He agreed. The ancient circle of trees was to be his final resting place.

Another friend named Ron, was also dying of AIDS. I told him what I was going to do with Kent's ashes and he asked me if I would take something of his to be buried. A few days later he gave me a box and asked me to open it before burying it. Thus, the idea of taking "ending things" to this great circle of trees as offerings began. The Heart of the Redwoods, that decayed center of a tree that I had found in that very circle of trees on my first trip to the redwoods, had become dried and lifeless, and seemed to want to go home as well.

During this time my great Aunt Ruby was nearing her end. She lived alone in a small wooden house with a garden where she grew vegetables and cucumbers that she made into pickles which she canned. Aunt Ruby had come into my life as she was nearing the end of her own.

"I and Harry," she used to say when she was about to tell a story. They were always "earthy" stories about hitching rides on trains for their honeymoon or rootin' through the dumps for things that they could use or maybe even sell during the depression. They never did make much money. She and Harry loved and lived an uncomplicated life and they never seemed to need more than that.

I told Aunt Ruby about my decision to take "remains" to the redwoods, and asked her if she would like me to take something of hers. "Will anyone ever find it?" she asked. "No," I answered. So she gave me a compact with a mirror and powder puff that Harry had given to her in the early 1930s.

During this time I made friends with another man who was dying. His name again, was John. I visited with John often as he neared his end. He was growing a pot plant that he was proud of and would point out its progress whenever I stopped by. Upon his death I was surprised to find that he had left me his plant. I dried the leaves and decided to take them to the redwoods as an offering from him.

This was the mid 1980s. Most of the gay people in the United States knew many others who had AIDS or had it themselves. So many of my friend died at that time.

Previously, I had found a wonderful tourmaline crystal which had been freshly brought up from the mines north of San Diego, in a box of assorted crystals for sale. When I picked it up it felt like a gyroscope twisting in my hands. It was so powerful! I showed it to a lady friend who was a psychic. Together we cupped it in our hands and her eyes widened with delight as our entwined hands twisted and danced with the energy of the crystal. It was a magnificent thing.

I wanted to make the crystal into an amulet signifying the Flame that I had seen with The Mountain. I envisioned a golden flame on the top and a silver spike on the bottom. I also wanted a writhing figure to represent Love. I would have that made in brass.

I had some gold from fillings that had been removed from my teeth as well as a gold ring which meant a lot to me. It was a "partnering ring" that Jon and I had bought for each other back in 1965 while I was still a materialistic programmer.

A friend of mine made jewelry and wanted to make the amulet. I gave her the gold to make the flame. She would provide the silver and brass.

I waited anxiously for the two weeks that it took her to make the amulet, but when I got the crystal back, the power was gone. The golden flame and the silver spike had "capped" the energy within the tourmaline. The brass figure of love was not attached so it didn't cause problems, but I was horrified. I didn't want to harm the crystal further by forcing the symbols off so I sat it on a shelf for awhile. Before long I decided to take it to the redwoods. The amulet would now be my offering to the forest. I could feel the energy of the trees reaching out to the crystal. I hoped that with time, the glue would deteriorate and leave the crystal free of the gold flame and silver spike.

Rodger wanted to join me on this journey to the Redwoods honoring Aunt Ruby and our friends.

He knew and loved Aunt Ruby. He also knew Kent and Ron who were to be remembered.

I still had the motor home so we travelled in style. It was good to be traveling with Rodger again. We did like each other very much. We decided that since we would be in Northern California we might as well go up into Oregon and do some sight-seeing as well.

The redwood trees of Northern California are among the oldest living things on earth. To those who open up to them there is a livingness about the trees that can be palpable. Take the time to study them and they can reveal great lessons about life. If you are fortunate, you can hear them speak. The Humboldt Redwoods in Northern California drew me back to them like a magnet, and they still had more magic to reveal.

We rented a campground, deep within the forest. It felt great to be back within the trees again. In the morning we went into the forest to find the special family of trees growing in a circle. I knew exactly where to enter the forest, however the trees themselves are in constant change. As they grow they fall over and grow again. The forest changes in major ways very often, and try though we may, we could not find the circle of trees.

After a while I became irritated. I came upon a scrawny group of small trees that were kind of growing in a circle. It was dry and the area within the circle had no vegetation, but I wanted to get on with our trip to Oregon so I decided to bring the offerings to this "less than grand" place the following day. Back at the road we marked carefully just where to enter the forest and took a compass reading so that we would know exactly where to go.

In the morning, as we were about to leave to go into the forest with our offerings, I became violently ill and had to stay in bed. After a few hours we decided that there was no way we were going to be able to go into the forest that day. We decided to continue our trip north and stop for the burial on our way home.

I began to feel better as soon as we left the forest and we had a very enjoyable trip up the coast. The beaches are filled with driftwood and wonderful rocks. I got some beautiful pictures and even a huge piece of driftwood which I brought back home and used in my garden for years until it just decayed away, much the pattern of the Northern California Redwood area.

When we got back to the Redwoods we set up our camp and made dinner. Then we gathered all of our mementos and prepared to enter the forest in the morning.

We stood at the edge of the road which we had marked earlier as our entry point. I wanted to dedicate our visit as we started into the forest so we smoked some of the pot that John, my dying friend, had left to me. The words, "*Well I'll be*" sounded in my mind. It was the voice of my dead friend.

Smiling, we took a compass reading and headed into the forest. This time we knew exactly where we were going. Rodger carried some of our offerings and I carried the rest. After a while, I realized that I had no idea where we were. There was no similarity between where we were and where we had been on our earlier visit. The straggly growth of trees growing in a circle was nowhere to be found. I asked Rodger to take a compass reading. It showed that we had been going in entirely the wrong direction. Grumbling a bit, we headed off using the new bearing.

Again I did not recognize the area and I took a reading from my own compass. It showed that we were heading in an entirely different direction. Frustrated, we followed the latest reading. After a while, I set my packages down and said, "We have the heart of the redwoods here, let's use it to show us the way." I took the withered center of the tree in my hands and stretched it out toward the forest. Sending energy through my fingers, I circled around until I found a "pull" in my hands. "It's over there," I exclaimed.

I sat the "Heart of the Redwoods" down upon the ground and I picked up the bundles. When I went to pick up the tree heart, it refused to go. There was a force between it and the ground that was magnetic. I felt as if it were saying, *"I'm home, leave me here!"* I did not want to leave it there because we were on flat, clear land with nothing to protect it from passers-by who might step on it. I began to weep; I really didn't want to leave it there.

"The Heart of the Redwoods." For years I had hung it on my wall as an art piece and referred to it by that name. It was only now that I was going to have to leave it that I finally realized what it was.

It had begun several thousand years earlier as pollen from a male flower was blown up through a giant Redwood tree in search of a female flower which grew only at the top of the trees. The pollen found a female flower and a cone was produced which contained at least 100 seeds. When the time was right the cone fell to the ground. Fronds from surrounding trees dropped to cover and protect the cone during the coming winter. As the cone dried, it opened to release the seeds. Most seeds were not fertile and very few survived. This one did however, and was the only one from the cone to grow into a giant redwood. First, the seed became a seedling, then grew upward and became a tree which in time had passed on its own offspring. Perhaps 2,000 years passed. The tree became a giant and grew old. Falling over from its own weight, it lay decaying until only the core center, the heart, was left to be taken home and used as a wall hanging before finding its way back home.

This I was going to have to leave, sitting thus on the ground, alone and unprotected. I decided to leave my amulet as a guard. The tourmaline crystal tipped with gold and silver would remain. Again tears flowed, for these things had meant a lot to me and I had so wanted to leave something of myself inside of the circle of trees.

Once before I had had a magic tourmaline crystal that I could not keep. Perhaps it is not for me to be able to keep such things.

We didn't have to walk far. It was only on the other side of a huge tree. In the redwoods, so much remains hidden "just around a tree." They are so very huge. As we walked around the tree we came upon the most amazing sight I could ever believe. Giant trees in a vast circle, all multistoried high, had fallen in toward each other leaving an enormous circle of massive tree root fans. Their tips were touching and overlapping one another in a gentle blending. The effect was like looking at spokes of a gigantic wheel. The great root systems around the circle had weakened the earth as the roots pulled out and another, outer ring of great trees, were leaning in toward the circle. Someday, they too, would fall in toward the center. It was like a giant "sink hole" of trees where an entire area of the forest was turning over and renewing itself.

The exact center of the trees was easy to find. They had grown, lived and fell over with just the right space to meet each other at the center. This was a place greater than my wildest dreams for my tributes! The forest itself had made a place for my offerings. Could it possibly have been less? I doubt it.

We made our way easily to the center of the fallen trees. There we opened our packages. First, we placed the ashes of my friend, Kent. Within the ashes we placed my Aunt Ruby's compact, open so the mirror was exposed. Then we opened the box that I had been carrying from Ron, my neighbor back home. There was a poem, a few other things, and some wildflower seeds. These I scattered around the trees.

Then I burst out laughing. The last thing in the box was a plastic heart saying, "Love" with a magnet on the back to stick it to a refrigerator. While trying to find the scrawny baby circle of trees by compass reading, the needle had been pulled by the force of Love. Love; the form that had surrounded the flame symbol not so far from that place, but so very long ago, had been guiding us all along. Thus it was that we had been led to this magnificent and holy place. Only through the power of this magnetic heart, my friend Ron's heart, would we ever have found this wonderful place of rebirth. We couldn't have asked for a more perfect burial ground.

We took careful compass readings as we left (unencumbered by a magnet) so that we could find our way back. I wanted to photograph this amazing scene. As with so many things within the redwoods, I was never able to find it again but I did carry several pounds of camera equipment all over the forest looking for it.

Rodger and I always remained good friends. Unfortunately he got caught up in the AIDS epidemic. It had gained full strength while we were relatively safe in Durango. Rodger was stoic about it and kept his sense of humor until the end. One good thing that came from this was that his daughter, Diana, came from Oakland to take care of him. Seeing him only a few times since he had run off to Durango with me, she finally got a chance to get to know her dad.

Rodger was always good for a laugh. A memory remains of a story that Diana giggled to me about going shopping with her father. "He was speeding his wheelchair up and down the isles like a mad man," she chuckled. Yup, that was Rodger.

In September of 1998 I made another visit to the Redwoods. I wanted to get away from the city and my job to just be with the forest and photograph the trees. I had just had an operation performed on my foot. I took my dog Sandy, who was becoming old. I knew that the deep trips within the forest were not to happen for us on this visit but I figured the trees themselves would show me where to enter the forest.

On the way up to the Redwoods I passed a nude beach where I enjoyed going on the weekends. I decided to take a beach rock with me to offer to the forest as a gift. I parked my truck and hiked down the steep trail to the beach. I was almost to the bottom when I spied three objects in the sand. I knew that these were what I was to take as my gift. I took my clothes off as I got to the beach. (It just didn't feel appropriate to do it clothed here.) Then I collected the three objects, put my clothes back on, hiked back up to the road and continued my trip.

The next day, as I entered the forest, I stopped to offer a blessing. I had brought a crystal with me (just a normal crystal this time), and I shined reflected rainbows into the trees.

Having thus blessed the forest I searched for a place where Sandy and I could enter the forest without having to climb too much. The place soon presented itself to us in the shape of a lightning-struck tree. It looked almost like an arrow saying, *"Here I am."*

We found a lovely grove of trees, perfect for photography. I took the crystal and hung it on a low hanging branch a little ways into the forest, far enough to make it private yet close enough so that I could see the flashes of crystal light. Then I took the three objects that I had brought from the beach and made a presentation in the center of the grove. It was only as I was placing them that I realized that I had a shell, a piece of redwood and a rock. Animal, vegetable, and mineral.

I enjoyed an afternoon of photography, then when I looked for the crystal that I had hung in the trees, it was nowhere to be found. Chuckling to myself, I could almost hear the forest saying, *"Mine."*

I photographed most of the following day in the grove. I could see rainbows glinting throughout the forest all day but I was never able to find the crystal again. I had finished shooting and was packing my camera equipment into the truck when I heard a voice saying, *"Accept my blessing."*

I turned and saw a tree that looked as if it had a great

opened mouth. There was a large section of bark slightly askew, that looked as if the tree was gesturing to me. I took out my camera again, set it up and shot the scene. The first shot I took was to be my "season card," for the year. With the caption of course of, "Accept my blessing."

It was only when I got home and developed the film that I realized that this tree had been communicating with me all day. How very expressive 'she' was. I had photographed the tree many times from several different angles throughout the day, mostly with other trees so she didn't really stand out. Each time the tree had assumed a different expression for my camera.

Leaving the forest, I noticed a bright light that kept flashing in my eyes. It was quite irritating, flashing back and forth into my eyes. Then I realized that it was reflections from a crystal that was hung from the mirror in the car in front of me. The rainbows that it sent to me were to continue for many miles, a blessing indeed, from the redwoods.

As the last trees of the forest passed away and open freeway began, there is a barn on the side of the road. On the side is painted in huge letters: *"Remember the magic."*

In August 2007, on a return trip with my friend Chiu from Taiwan I saw the sign again. My memory was incorrect, the sign reads - - - "Don't forget the magic."

Sleepy dog in the Redwoods

"Please accept my blessing."

And - -

Afterword

From the day I met John, the Hippie, I began to follow my heart into an ever-changing journey through the lives of this story and more. Following my heart is, and will continue to be, the compass of my life.

Spending four months in Europe when I was a hippie taught me that I could get along in a country where I didn't know the language. After learning this lesson I have ventured into Asia, spending months in areas that I would never have dared to visit alone before. Thailand, China, South Korea, India, Tibet and Taiwan; even back to Europe again. I have friends in all of those countries now. I have adventured in ways that Michael the programmer would never have thought possible.

The hippies used to say, "If you have something, give it away; if it comes back to you it's yours, if it doesn't, it didn't belong to you anyway." I was to give my house and all of my belongings away. I quit a well paying and stable job, left the vast majority of my friends behind and walked into the future with nothing but myself. I did not know what I was going to do or where I was to go when I let it all go, but a pathway was always unfolding in front of me.

Since then I have owned (with Rodger), three houses, a trailer and a motor home. In the years that have followed, I have seldom gone without food or shelter and always seem to have enough money. As with all of my lives, I also have many wonderful friends. I gave everything away, now all that I want is at my fingertips.

My journeys are not over, but it seems that I have finally found home.

MF/BB

Michaelsrainbow.com

www.ingramcontent.com/pod-product-compliance
Lightning Source LLC
Chambersburg PA
CBHW071454040426
42444CB00008B/1333